BEST OF
BORA BORA

Create the vacation of a lifetime

Gloria Altus & Melinda Altus-Richardson

Bora Bora Island Guide
Visit our website at www.BoraBoraIslandGuide.com

Printed in the United States of America

First Printing: March 2018
Updated February 2019

ISBN-9781976930270

CONTENTS

THE VACATION OF A LIFETIME

B ora Bora is unlike any other place on earth. A large, protected lagoon surrounds a verdant, volcanic peak creating a vision so pleasing that it has been titled *Pearl of the Pacific* and named *Most Beautiful Island in the World.* This turquoise and emerald isle offers luxury, tranquility, and out-of-this-world experiences in lush tropical surrounds. There are activities to challenge your comfort zone, enliven your senses, inspire colorful memories, and send you home with a renewed zest for life.

For most people, Bora Bora is no ordinary vacation; it's a bucket list trip which takes years to save for. Often, it's reserved for a special celebration and you want everything to be perfect. But when visiting a place for the first time, we usually make mistakes or learn what we should have done and find ourselves noting what to do differently next time. We don't want you to have that experience as most travelers don't get a dress rehearsal for Bora Bora; it's a once in a lifetime adventure.

"Best of Bora Bora" is packed with practical information dispelling the many mysteries surrounding this far-off, legendary isle. The illuminating discussions and comparisons will help clarify choices about when to go and where to sleep, eat and play in such a unique environment. Your vacation time is precious and it's not a cheap destination, so you'll enjoy double the delight by spending your dollars on the best. You'll also be pleased to discover that you don't always have to pay the *most* money to have the *best* time.

Let us guide you through the most important things to know and consider when planning, booking, and living your dream. Every choice we discuss contributes to a brilliant vacation, so this book is designed to be read cover to cover. We share experiences, strategies, and tips with the aim of ensuring that you enjoy everything that's best about Bora Bora – on your honeymoon, anniversary, bucket-list trip or vacation of a lifetime – the first time you go! Welcome to Paradise...

THE BEST TIME TO GO
TO BORA BORA

FOR WEATHER

The weather can play an important role in your experience as most of your vacation hours will be enjoyed in the amazing outdoors.

Bora Bora is a sublime setting to chill out from the usual rush and sync with natural rhythms. Temperatures are warm most of the year, so you can get around unencumbered by layers of clothing, laze on white-sand beaches, jump into the lagoon from your bungalow, and engage in a diversity of exciting activities. This enchanting island invites visitors to come into their senses and go home feeling refreshed.

At the beginning of planning it's important to know that the weather has a significant influence on your vacation experience as *most of your island hours will be enjoyed in the amazing outdoors.* And not just on the beach or at the pool! Most resort restaurants open to the air and your romantic thatched-roof bungalow will have glass sliding doors that open wide to an awesome deck which is likely to be your favorite habitat for the week.

Getting around your resort will be a pleasure if you pick the right time to go. The luxury resorts are spread over vast areas which are connected by paths that wander through lush tropical gardens and lead to long wooden pontoons for accessing overwater villas. (We once had a site-visitor enquire if they had to swim to their bungalow!) There are long distances between resort facilities and many of the bungalows. This adds to the feeling of luxury and tranquility but gives more exposure to the elements. The best resorts all offer a "pick-up" and "drop-off" service in golf carts and some also provide the independence of bicycles, which are also fun to ride. But the grounds and views are so gorgeous that strolling around is delightful, providing it's not too hot or wet.

Getting around Bora Bora island will be a novel experience too. Most transport is by boat which means you have closer exposure to the both the weather and the beauty.

We've been to Bora Bora in *all* seasons and had a wonderful time. But to enjoy the very *best* of Bora Bora we recommend going at the time of the year when the weather is right for you. Here's a description of the typical weather in each season:

Winter Weather in Bora Bora

Bora Bora is in the southern hemisphere, so winter is in June, July and August. During these months the prevailing trade-winds moderate the air temperature, the humidity is at its lowest, and the lagoon is a couple degrees cooler. The sun's angled position in the sky makes this the most suitable season for fair skinned folk to safely build a golden glow without having to watch the clock closely.

Winter may also be the preferred time for those who live in cooler climates and dislike humidity. Although there's always the option to turn on air conditioning in your bungalow, most other places you will hang out at won't be airconditioned. Those who wilt in tropical heat will have much more fun in the winter months as an island vacation is about enjoying the glorious environment, even while sitting on the deck of your bungalow or at a restaurant.

Although there's more rain in Bora Bora over the summer months this *is* the tropics, so it can rain all year round, even in winter. That's why the vegetation is so lush and green. In winter the sky is likely to be less cloudy and short rain showers tend to fall in the morning or overnight. These night-time showers are good. If it rains overnight this usually means that the next day will be clear and sunny.

Luckily, even when it's cloudy or raining, the lagoon is still a brilliant blue. The water temperature is a few degrees cooler because: more ocean-water flows into the lagoon; wind can make the lagoon water a little choppy; and the current in the lagoon can be stronger.

Those coming from a cooler climate will like the water temperate but if you are from a warmer climate you might find it a little cooler than expected. On our last visit, while we were out on a lagoon excursion with a floating bar experience, we heard a couple from Arizona complaining that they were getting cold in the water. The water is certainly not cold, but it is noticeably cooler compared to the summer months. I prefer visiting Bora Bora when the lagoon is warmer as I feel the cold and enjoy the lagoon. The winter water temperature limits the length of time it's comfortable for me to stay in.

If you decide to book your vacation during winter and feel the cold, bring a couple jackets or cardigans and a light wind proof/waterproof jacket. On cloudy or rainy days, and in the evenings, it can be necessary to put on an extra layer to feel comfortable. If you are out on the lagoon or visit a restaurant with air-conditioning, you may be glad to have some warmth.

There are a couple of other, less thought of, aspects you may wish to consider when deciding which season to go to Bora Bora. Bora Bora can turn on grand sunsets. During the winter months only about one evening out of four has a flaming-red sky. The best sunsets occur more frequently in November and we have a huge appreciation for these spectacles. We've also noticed that there are not as many bright, tropical flowers about during the cooler winter months.

June, July, and August are peak season in Bora Bora so if you decide to go in these months it's advisable to book as far ahead as possible – preferably a year ahead – to ensure you secure the accommodation and flights you want. With more tourists visiting, accommodation rates are higher. If you prefer to visit Bora Bora when both the weather and the lagoon are warmer, you can save money – or spend your money on a better resort or bungalow – by vacationing in off-peak or shoulder season in Bora Bora.

Spring and Autumn Weather in Bora Bora

The spring months of September, October and November; and the autumn months of March, April, and May; have a good balance of weather. Spring and autumn are milder seasons. These are our favorite times to go to Bora Bora for the best all-round *weather and water* experience. There are no trade winds to cool down the air and lagoon but there's also not the intense humidity of the summer rainy season months. We can walk around the resort comfortably and never need to turn on dehydrating air-conditioning in our bungalow. The window for saving during shoulder season months has been decreasing each year as the increased popularity of these months encourages resorts to extend their peak season prices into May, October and November. If you want to go in spring or autumn book your trip as far in advance as you can. Ask your travel agent about which dates remain in shoulder season. You can save a significant amount of money by going a week earlier or a week later to avoid peak season prices.

Summer Weather in Bora Bora

The summer months in Bora Bora Bora – December, January, and February – are the hottest and wettest months of the year. The humidity is high, and both the air and lagoon temperatures are warm. Summer is the rainy season and there may be frequent showers though they are usually light and pass quickly. It's best to wear sandals or thongs that won't spoil if they get wet. Bring a rain jacket/coat or you may end up walking around in a huge, hooded, plastic bag (poncho) that the resorts give out and is very difficult to dry and re-use!

The warm summer months are our favorite time for enjoying the famous lagoon as the water temperature is so bath-like we can swim and snorkel for hours and not become cold. We also like the exotic feel of the fragrant, humid air. There's something wonderful about being able to throw on a skimpy dress to go to breakfast in the morning and stroll around the grounds in the balmy evening with a light breeze caressing bare skin.

Keep in mind that everything is 'open' and you will be walking in heat and humidity during the middle of the day. It's vital to bring light, loose clothing and plenty of sun protection – in the form of sunscreen and throw-over shirts – as the sun is at its strongest over summer. But if you come from a warm climate you will thrive in Bora Bora over the summer months. Even when the sky turns overcast, the lagoon gleams an iridescent bright-turquoise and, because there are less visitors, the island is so peaceful.

Summer is low season in Bora Bora, which means there are practical advantages to going then. There's no competition for airfares so they are more readily available and cheaper, and the resorts offer cheaper prices. We recommend that you collaborate with the specialist travel agency we use. The staff know Bora Bora, are aware of the very best bargains on offer, and have the influence to negotiate cheaper prices. This is the best time of year to get extras thrown in and there's a greater chance of being given an upgrade, especially if you have the best agent on your team.

FOR ENTERTAINMENT

Heiva Festival

The Heiva festival, held in Tahiti and Bora Bora during July, is a month-long celebration of Polynesian history and culture. This is the biggest event of the year so it's an exciting time to travel to Tahiti. The most popular events are the traditional singing and dancing performances which tell legends and stories. The groups rehearse all year and their costumes are exceptional. If you go to Bora Bora in July, plan to stop a couple days on the main island of Tahiti to see some events there. Then fly across to Bora Bora to catch some of the local dance teams competing for first place over several days. Other interesting events in Bora Bora include outrigger-canoe racing, coconut preparation, and banana harvesting.

During June the locals prepare for the Heiva by erecting traditional, thatched-roof fares, decorated with shells and tropical plants. These are judged for design and authenticity, and are used for restaurants which serve delicious, moderately-priced food for lunch and dinner, until late at night. It's a colorful atmosphere so, if you want to have most participation - and don't need top luxury - consider staying on the main island of Bora Bora.

Hawaiki Nui Va'a

Canoe racing is a legacy of the courageous, seafaring expeditions which the ancient Polynesians set out on; following the sun and the stars; to discover and populate the scattered Pacific islands. Today it's the national sport in Tahiti. We see boys playing in canoes, in deep water, when quite small; and young men vigorously rowing after work each day. The biggest race of the year, Hawaiki Nui Va'a is held each year in November. This spectacular race has 3 separate legs, between 4 Society Islands, over 3 days. It comes to a muscle-rippling finish at award winning, 2mile long Matira Beach in Bora Bora.

Christmas and New Year

The spirit of Christmas can also be found far out in the Pacific. It's a fantastic time to take a break from the yearly holiday routine and have a white-sand Christmas. In Bora Bora, the resorts glisten with festive decorations and present a big feast with French wine flowing. The entertainment is a spectacular display of vibrant, Polynesian dancing.

One Christmas we cruised around Tahiti for 10 days. Our boat had 7 sparkling Christmas trees and I didn't have to put the balls up or take tinsel down from any. Best of all, I spent Christmas day in the lagoon and yet succulent turkey arrived on my plate as I sat at a ceremonious table; chatting with family and friends. Being able to walk to our cabin bed each evening was a bonus. We had the most wonderful Yuletide of our lives!

New Year is also a special occasion in Bora Bora. Each luxury resort holds a huge banquet with a lively traditional dance show for entertainment. The new year is ushered in by several displays of fireworks over the lagoon. To be at a resort which hosts fireworks, enquire about whether the one you're considering has them. Some locals head out in their boats and float in the lagoon to enjoy the fireworks. Visitors can party lagoon-side, with the locals, over at the Bora Bora Yacht club. New Year is a great time to self-cater on your deck as delicious pork, duck and seafood platters can be purchased from Chin-Lee's in Vaitape, especially for the occasion.

If you want to escape from the cold (and the obligations of Christmas) head to Bora Bora for a warm, white-sand Christmas and a spectacular new year!

Now that you know your preferred time to go, there are important things to be aware of for booking.

BEST TIME TO BOOK

Bora Bora is not a 'last minute' package deal destination.

This is a very small island with limited flight and accommodation options. If you want to experience the best of Bora Bora by having your first preference of resort and room type and enjoy the most exclusive activities, for the best price, you must book as far in advance as possible.

Jump on a Deal

Bora Bora resorts offer deals at certain times to encourage more bookings. When they have sold enough rooms, for the designated period, they pull the good rate. You may talk about a resort rate with your travel agent on one day but when you call back the next day to book it, the offer may no longer be available for your agent to secure. We had this happen with our booking for the Four Seasons on a recent vacation. The offered rate was stay 4 and get the 5th night free. When our final itinerary was ready, and we confirmed the booking with our agent, she discovered that Four Seasons was not allowing that special offer anymore – they can change their rates without notice! Because we were booking through Pacific for Less, a specialist agency which has built connections with the resorts, Jennifer was able to speak with Four Seasons and get them to honor the special rate that we had intended to book. This would not always be possible. Resorts can change their rates without notice so the outcome of a situation like this would not always benefit the client. But having such a dedicated agent, who has good rapport with the resorts, certainly helped us. Make sure you take advantage of a special offer that comes your way, without delay!

Booking for Peak Season

Those intending to travel during peak season must book ahead. Peak season in Bora Bora falls over both American and European breaks, so everything gets booked out. The months on either side of peak season fill up quickly too. If you're wanting to travel to Bora Bora during June, July or August; start planning well in advance. Booking a year ahead is ideal.

Book excursions as soon as you know which ones you want to take. During the busy months the most exclusive tours do sell out as they cater for such small numbers. Arrange any special events, such as a private romantic dinner at your resort, as far ahead as you can, or there may not be availability.

Booking for Low Season & Shoulder Season

Traveling to Bora Bora over less popular months will save you money and allow more freedom to book closer to your travel date. We have booked trips within 2-3 months of departure and secured reasonable airfares and managed to get accommodation deals with free nights and extras thrown in. Although availability of rooms and resorts is more limited, by being flexible it's possible to create a wonderful trip. We recommend planning a vacation for low season or shoulder season at least 6 months in advance to secure your best options.

Be aware that the best tours, that take limited numbers of people, will sell out at any time of year. Secure any special activities and excursions before you depart for your trip.

Offers to look out for:

- Fourth or fifth night free
- Free daily breakfast
- Honeymoon and anniversary specials that include romantic experiences like a flowerbed and couple's massage
- Half board included
- Complimentary massages with a required number of nights booked
- Advance purchase with 30-60% off

Now that you know the need to book ahead, you'll be keen to pick a hotel. Most people have difficulty choosing a Bora Bora resort as they think that there must be only one "best" one. They are concerned about getting it right because they're going for a special occasion and making a big financial investment.

We understand that it's not an easy decision and want to end the confusion by spelling out which resort is best for what. You'll discover that each resort is unique and offers some different experiences; plus, you don't always have tò pay top dollar to have a top stay. The next chapter will give you clarity about which resort in Bora Bora will be best for you.

WHERE TO STAY IN BORA BORA

*Where you stay in Bora Bora will have more impact
on your vacation than any other decision.*

FOR THE BEST BEACH & SCENIC SURROUNDS

Each Luxury resort is set along a private white-sand beach on a small island in the lagoon. The resort you choose will give you access to one of the world's most admired beaches, which is exclusively for the use of guests.

Having easy beach access (and spectacular lagoon views) is the basic reason to stay at a resort. There is only one public beach, Matira on the main island, and it can take time and effort to get there from other areas of Bora Bora. The resorts are designed for guests to enjoy most of their time lolling around the beautiful grounds. The beach, its outlook, and the water equipment available, may provide much of the fun on your vacation.

Accommodation at Bora Bora resorts is mostly, or all, overwater bungalows. This gives guests the convenient choice of sunning and swimming straight from their bungalows and means there are always empty deckchairs on the serene beaches. Lounging on the deck of an overwater bungalow is immense fun but we find that a perfect beach adds another dimension to a vacation. In Bora Bora the exquisite strips of white sand are never crowded like in Hawaii, Europe or the Caribbean; in fact, sometimes you'll feel like you're the only ones on a beach.

*Each resort beach is unique.
Compare the experiences the best resorts offer:*

Bora Bora Four Seasons

The service and outlook on the Four Seasons beach are as good as it gets on the planet! Each time I strolled onto the Four Seasons beach there was a neat row of padded sun-lounges waiting right at the water's edge. When I glanced towards one, a beaming beach-waiter instantly appeared with a purpose-designed towel under his arm, unrolled it, spread it out, and tucked it neatly under the cushions. If the sky-blue umbrella was folded up, he inquired if I would like to have it opened. After ensconcing me in comfort, he asked what he could bring me to drink.

Cups of water, clinking with ice, flowed freely all day. Beer and cocktails appeared like visions. When hunger distracted me from the views, our minder appeared with a menu that offered a wide choice of snacks, meals and salads. We picnicked lavishly on the beach, viewing the turquoise water just beyond our toes, and the grandeur of Mt Otemanu across the lagoon. In the afternoon, as the sun sunk lower in the sky, I asked for the umbrella to be moved to the side. Our beach waiter lifted it like a feather, grinning, as if it was pleasing to attend to my comforts.

The swimming pool is another blissful attraction at Four Seasons beach. As Bora Bora's lagoon-water rates highly for purity in regular stringent testing and temperatures are pleasant all year, I prefer to swim in the salt water. Yet even if you never take a dip, the visual appeal of the swimming pool sets the scene for soaking in pleasure on a luxurious lounge nearby. A romantic row of thatched-roof, comfy cabanas adds romance to the scene and provides privacy.

The pool lies at the edge of the beach, like a giant wave that has been washed ashore; with Bora Bora Island, the lagoon and a perfectly manicured beach displayed up front, as if on a huge canvas. It's an amazing "pinch-me-is-this-real" place to hang out. Bora Bora beaches are *all* beautiful but this one has the most spectacular scenery, setup, and friendly service from local islanders.

Four Seasons has plenty of complimentary kayaks and stand-up paddle boards and is the only resort with wave-runners for hire. The beach has small pieces of broken coral in the water and you can protect your feet by wearing water-shoes when entering. You'll find attractive ones, easily available online. Take some with you to have the best time.

Conrad Nui

The Conrad Nui has the superb advantage of being the only Bora Bora resort located on a natural beach. (The other resorts had to build the sand up to create theirs.) This secluded resort is tucked away on a lush green motu which was created when the volcano that formed Bora Bora, erupted. The extraordinary beach and pool are backed by a steep lush hillside and one end of the beach is bordered by dramatic lava rocks that emerged from the depths of the earth. Though there's no view to the main island from the beach this is offset by the feeling of tranquility - and what this beach *does* have!

We frolicked on the Conrad's gorgeous beach, snorkeling, stand-up paddle boarding and trying out the pedalos. Although we had a large swimming pool on the deck of our Presidential Overwater Villa, the beach was so inviting we chose to enjoy that during the day. Our stay was in high season yet there were only several others enjoying the beach each time we went. Most guests, not in their bungalow or out on excursion, were lounging around the artistic pool and bar area. The stretch of perfect white sand beach is so long that, no matter how busy the resort is, you will always find a quiet spot all for yourself.

The soft, sandy bottom slopes gently from the edge, to a depth that was great for swimming, and then became deeper. The first time we donned fins and snorkels we were thrilled to discover abundant living coral, with colorful fish, just several meters from the beach. We explored the entire area and found coral, with neon fish shyly darting in and out, growing around the overwater bungalows and extending the length of the resort. We could even sit in shallow water at the edge, with inquisitive fish darting around our feet. Nui guests can have one of the best Bora Bora snorkeling experiences – without leaving the resort.

There was no food or drink service to sun-lounges on the beach, just someone to help coach how to use the variety of water-craft. This was fine. It was a novelty to eat and have refreshments at the intimate nooks which have been cleverly designed into the pool-bar or relax at the feet-in-the-sand restaurant. Both are just a few steps away and overlook the beach.

Intercontinental Thalasso

The Intercontinental Resort has a prime position on the eastern ring of motus that form a protective barrier around the Bora Bora lagoon. While lazing on the beach we could gaze directly across the lagoon to Mt Otemanu. The main island seems so close that professional photographers like to frame the signature peak from the Thalasso beach.

For several years we displayed this wondrous view as our website header, showing the beach in the foreground, decked out with inviting sun-lounges under shady pandanus umbrellas. We loved the luxurious feeling of being on that beach – even though our vacation was in summer with unpredictable rain showers. On a recent vacation we stayed at Four Seasons and were so captivated by the dramatic angle of the mountain on show from their well-serviced beach that it became our favorite.

The Intercontinental Thalasso beach has a soft, sandy floor below very clear water that's a surreal light-turquoise. It has the added interest of a small, shallow inner-lagoon with some coral and fish which provides a place for beginner snorkelers to have fun while they get comfortable in their goggles and snorkel.

At this resort you can enjoy the indulgence of relaxing back on a sun-lounge or beach chair, right on the sand, and have drinks, smoothies, snacks, and light meals brought by the waiters from South Beach Bar. The wait staff are mostly French expatriates and we experienced the good service that the Intercontinental has a reputation for.

The beach is also a hub for activities. Complimentary water equipment includes stand-up paddle boards, kayaks, and pedalos. Around lunch time the beach-boys offer cultural experiences, with demonstrations on how to make the most popular local dish or weave hats and baskets. In the early afternoon there's an opportunity to meet the sting rays. These curious creatures come right up to the water's edge when the beach-boy feeds them with fish, at 2pm. Guests can watch from the sand or wade in to pat these friendly locals. The Intercontinental is the only resort providing this "must have" experience, which is included in most lagoon excursions.

Pearl Beach

The unforgettable view from the sand at Pearl Beach Resort shows the exact *opposite side* of the main island to that seen from the Thalasso beach. This beach has a magical atmosphere which put me in a dreamy state of meditation. As well as sun-lounges, there are delightful 2-person hammocks strung between palms. If you lie in one of those, with your love or a book you love, you won't want to leave.

We also have a soft spot for this beach because we enjoyed a day with the guide who was leading hikes into the wild inner isle to discover remains of old villages. He revealed that from Pearl Beach you can clearly see the outline of the ancient Valley of the Kings (which was part of his intriguing tour).

The beach is backed by a scattering of bungalows and shady, tropical gardens that make this flat, volcanic moto beautiful. The distinctively Polynesian beach-bungalows are dotted along the edge of the sand and you step straight out of these onto one of the most romantic beaches in the world. They have been artfully constructed and decorated with natural materials so are imbued with an island ambiance. But (unlike Robinson Crusoe's) their lovely outdoor bathrooms have modern conveniences. This resort is a step down in "stars" but it has a tropical island resonance that those who don't demand top luxury will love.

Le Meridien

Le Meridien was the first resort to be built on the eastern chain of coral motus so its private beach boasts spectacular views directly across the lagoon to the rocky outcrop of Mount Otemanu. It's a surprise to arrive and find just how close the mountain is, because wide angled photographs don't show the real proximity.

Le Meridien's lovely white sand gives way to an inner lagoon at the side. Guests have a choice of swimming from the beach, bathing in the shallow shelter of the inner-lagoon or dipping in the pool which has a prime position next to the beach.

Le Meridien's beach has generous shade from clumps of palm trees. Although the resort is mostly comprised of overwater bungalows, there's a scattering of beach bungalows, with modern interiors, nestled amongst palms around the inner areas of the beach.

This resort has been designed to give the restaurants fantastic views across the idyllic beach to the lagoon and mountain. When you stay at le Meridien you know you're in Bora Bora from the moment you open your eyes in the morning.

Sofitel Private Island

The Sofitel Private Island was originally an extension of Marara Beach Resort so was one of the first hotels to be built in Bora Bora. The newer large 5-star resorts have been constructed with luxurious rooms and vast grounds, but Sofitel Private Island has an exclusivity all of its own and when discussing "best beaches" it must get a mention. While the strip of sand is not as long as the beaches at most other resorts there's a special aura around this curved beach.

We celebrated with a private lunch under the shade of a palm, right near the water's edge. For over 2 hours we savored 5 delicious courses accompanied by matching wines, yet we simply *couldn't take our eyes off the view*! The water surrounding this tiny motu is a myriad of blue colors and mysterious Mt Otemanu looks down from above, so close across a narrow passage of lagoon. Years later, we still refer to this experience as the "lunch of our lives".

From the beach, guests can row a kayak or a Polynesian canoe around to the back of the motu and snorkel leisurely in one of the most popular coral gardens in Bora Bora. This gave us a most pleasurable afternoon as, unlike on an excursion, we were the only ones there.

If you're coming to Bora Bora to see the famous beaches but don't want to pay top dollar, at this resort, you can have an overwater bungalow with a mountain view, quite close to the beach. You'll also have a glorious 360-degree panorama of the lagoon from the hilltop. You can also take the free shuttle-boat across to the mainland and walk (15 minutes) down to 2-mile-long Matira Beach if you want to have more sand.

FOR ACCESSIBILITY TO THE MAIN ISLAND

By looking at a map of Bora Bora Island, you may assume that the large island in the center is the big deal, the main attraction! But when choosing your resort and planning activities, it's important to understand that, to experience the sublime joys of this miracle of nature, you must get out onto the lagoon and its sandy motus.

The best resorts in Bora Bora are not located on the main island, they're set on small motus (islands) surrounding the lagoon. Logistically, this means they can only be reached by the resort's scheduled shuttle-boat or booking a water taxi. Such an exclusive location provides the tranquility that many folk are seeking for a perfect vacation. These resorts are like Disney parks, pampering adults with a choice of interesting restaurants and activities on hand; it's not even necessary to leave!

So, if you're planning the vacation of a lifetime and want to enjoy the very *best of Bora Bora*, unless you are a geography teacher or an avid hiker, you may not want go tripping across to the main island, except on excursion. You may prefer to play around your amazing resort or be out on the lagoon with the main island as a backdrop for your activities.

- The main island has only one beach; lovely, long, white-sand Matira. This is the only public beach in Bora Bora.
- The transport hub on the mainland is at tiny Vaitape village which has banks, a post office and a variety of small shops and galleries.
- There are a few other points of interest around the island for those who are keen to explore but some of these can only be reached by a 4WD jeep.

Most visitors who want to see the mainland will get more enjoyment from viewing the sights on a tour with a local guide who gives interesting snippets from history and present-day life. You can choose between an on-land Circle Island Tour or an adventurous 4WD Tour which heads into the rugged inland.

However, we know that some visitors want a different style of Bora Bora vacation. They do want to have the freedom to eat at different restaurants, explore the main island, and get a taste of local life. One of the comments we hear from first-time travelers to Bora Bora is that they didn't realize how isolated their resort would be. So, it's important to understand that if you want to feel free to come and go as you please, you must take this into account when choosing your ideal accommodation.

Some resorts offer the best of both worlds while others seem to make it hard to leave. Here are the best resorts to stay at *if being able to come and go easily* is a factor for you:

Conrad Nui

Conrad offers guests a more frequent shuttle service than other 5-star resorts on a motu, and the boat goes directly to Vaitape village. This gives quick access to small shops and cafes in the main village on Bora Bora. From Vaitape it's just a $10 taxi ride to go and explore the popular Matira Beach area. It's easy to catch a taxi at the Vaitape wharf (Bora Bora's "Central Station"). But, if you wish, you can ask reception to have a cab waiting for you when the boat docks. Before heading out to dine at a restaurant, ask reception to make the arrangements as all the best restaurants on the main island offer a free pick-up service from and back to the wharf.

Sofitel Private Island

Private Island guests are surrounded by some of the best scenery in Bora Bora and they also enjoy an on-call shuttle to ferry them the short distance to and from the Sofitel Marara Beach resort on the mainland. It's the most convenient service offered by any resort. Sofitel guests also have the privilege of being able to row a kayak or canoe around to the back of the motu and freely explore the Aquarium, the most well-known coral gardens in Bora Bora.

Marara Beach Resort costs less and is located on the main island, in walking distance to other eating places and Matira Beach. But the Private Island offers more luxury and privacy and is very reasonably priced.

Intercontinental Thalasso

Intercontinental hotels run a frequent, free, shuttle service between the motu resort, Thalasso and its sister resort, Le Moana at Matira Beach. Thalasso is a good choice if you want the best of both Bora Bora worlds. You can stay in luxury out on a motu and enjoy the freedom of having easy access to the mainland and other eating places.

Intercontinental Le Moana

Located right on Matira Beach, Le Moana offers less luxury but has a charming, Polynesian ambiance. It was the first Bora Bora resort we stayed at and I still recall how fascinated I was by the lovely interior design of our bungalow which displayed the splendid skills of traditional artisans. This resort hasn't changed much over the years since it opened and there's something wonderful about that. It has remained authentically Polynesian and evokes a nostalgia for simpler times when inspired travelers came to see the blue lagoon before Bora Bora became the playground of the rich and famous. Le Moana's unique situation next to the only public beach, which is popular with both locals and visitors, makes the area outside its gate lively. There's a choice of cafes and restaurants just a few steps away.

From the Matira area you can get to Vaitape by bus or taxi for about $10. It's also easy to be picked up for excursions or by complimentary restaurant shuttles. The motu resorts schedule their last shuttle for 9 or 10 o'clock at night so by staying on the mainland you avoid these curfews which can lead to ending a meal hurriedly for a dash back to the boat dock.

IF YOU WANT A COUPLE'S RESORT

You've chosen the right destination. Bora Bora is practically a *couple's island!* Happy couples on honeymoon are 80% of vacationers in Bora Bora and many others are couples celebrating anniversaries or birthdays. The luxury resorts are dedicated to hosting perfect honeymoons and romantic vacations. They offer extraordinary experiences and you can make special requests to have fantasies fulfilled. Some resorts have staff dedicated to creating magic moments for couples and even offer romance menus. A good specialist Tahiti travel agent can arrange for lovely perks and experiences to be added in to create a whole vacation package.

The luxury resorts understand that couples require a romantic ambiance. Most have created areas especially for children and provide activities to keep them happily engaged. This is a win/win situation. Couples can relax around the resort *and* a whole family can vacation in Bora Bora and have a marvelous time! It gives parents the space to have some rare, high-quality couples time, without being interrupted by their offspring.

Very few parents bring their children to Bora Bora and it seems that only those with impeccable parenting styles do. During all our vacations we have never seen or heard an "out of place" child "acting up" around Bora Bora! On the contrary, we've been impressed by nostalgic scenes such as a little one totally absorbed in playing with her small toys next to the pool, while mummy relaxes; or a family of four out in formation together, on paddle-boards. Each time we've felt a warm and fuzzy response!

In contrast, at resorts on the main island of Tahiti, we have been annoyed by noisy, boisterous kids having fun around the swimming pools. It's been during times when school is out in France. If there's a few French families staying with children, the kids gravitate to the pool and naturally they get excited which leads to horse-play, and noise levels rise. From hard experience, we suggest you avoid Papeete hotels during the periods of European & American vacations.

If the non-presence of children is a critical factor when choosing your Bora Bora resort, we suggest that you pick a top luxury hotel. The pricing automatically deters most families. They're likely to choose Le Meridien or Pearl Beach which are more affordable. Le Meridien encourages families with youngsters to stay in their beach bungalows which provide very suitable accommodation as they're set back from the main lagoon. Pearl Beach has a scattering of on-land villas, lots of shady areas for kids to play under tropical vegetation, and a mini golf course to entertain.

If you don't need to stay 5-star but want peace and privacy ... with *no* possibility of a child in sight or sound ... Sofitel Private Island has the distinction of being the only resort in Bora Bora that has a no-child policy in place. It's for safety reasons because there's no boat on call after midnight which would create a problem in the case of a medical emergency.

The Private Island is a very small resort in a fantastic location. You're cut off from any bustle on the mainland and away from the water traffic that serves the strip of luxury resorts on the eastern chain of coral motus. Yet it's just a couple of minutes to the mainland with the complimentary shuttle-boat that's on-call until late at night. Another significant geographical aspect of this boutique resort is the jaw-dropping 360 degrees view from the hilltop; it's a photographer's dream.

This was one of the first hotels in Bora Bora. The bungalows are modest compared to those at the 5-star resorts and Sofitel has maintained a distinctly Polynesian theme which adds to the sense of calm that surrounds this unique resort. You can choose between a very intimate villa - set high up amongst trees on the hillside with wide views over the most sensational part of the lagoon - or be in an overwater bungalow with extraordinary views across to Mount Otemanu and around the multiple, blue hues of the lagoon. The hillside villas are one of the quietest, most private choices for accommodation in Bora Bora. However, if you have your heart set on an OWB there are far fewer here than at the larger resorts. Tranquility abounds at the Sofitel.

These luxury resorts focus on couple's vacations:

Conrad Nui

Conrad's completely refurbished overwater bungalows are designed with the perfect space for couples to feel like they're in an intimate, love nest. We fell in love at first sight and during our stay heard other guests gushing about the delights of their villas too.

The bungalows have spacious new decks equipped with every comfort you need to lay back (for a week), gaze across the blue lagoon to the horizon, and forget that any other world exists. You can cool down in your own pool (if you wish to have one) or descend the ladder to the lagoon and view the fantastic, underwater scenery.

The bed is the centerpiece of a villa and you wake up to see water all the way to the horizon (if you ask for the right villa). Each has a luxurious bathroom that gleams with fabulous, sparkling, new fittings. Sliding doors can close off the bedroom at whim and there are separate doors through to the shower and toilet at the back of the bungalow. This gives more privacy in the loo than any other overwater bungalow we've seen in Bora Bora.

All the eye-pleasing interiors at the elegant Conrad resort have a romantic "close to nature" feel. The imaginative use of color, shape, and natural materials provide a perfect background for gazing into the eyes of your beloved and being totally in the present. You'll have this ambiance around your bungalow, the restaurants, the pool with comfortable nooks, and the trendy, overwater bar.

Four Seasons Resort

Four Seasons was the last resort to be built in Bora Bora. As the stylish overwater bungalows were cleverly laid out on two pontoons there's more space between each villa and they're angled to provide the most privacy of any Bora Bora overwater villas for couples. During our stay we didn't hear or see the neighbors on their deck and we joyfully jumped from our private pontoon without neighbors peering on.

These bungalows have a separate living area but the only time we sat in the cushioned chairs was to fill out paperwork on arrival. Much of the fun of an over-water bungalow is being outside on the deck with the lagoon all around. So we really appreciated the level of privacy we had on our perfect-sized and positioned deck at Four Seasons. If you are far enough from shore, the mosquitoes won't come out over salt water, so you can also relax outside in the evening.

The 3 lovely bathroom areas had luxurious touches including: high quality products in the shower and by the basins, a scrubber cloth on the bath, 2 types of slippers under the basins, and robes in easy reach on hooks. It felt so welcoming. On our first morning we discovered that we could sit in the oversized, almost square bath, with the wall of wooden shutters to the blue lagoon wide open, without being seen.

The design of these bungalows is dreamy.

St Regis Resort

St Regis boasts the largest single story, overwater bungalows in Tahiti; each providing a generous 1500 square feet of extraordinary accommodation. They're more deserving of the name palace than bungalow or villa. There are a couple of strategically placed small, square windows down to the lagoon to remind guests they're in an *overwater* palace! The size of each room is very large and, along with the furnishings, suggests the kind of luxury that was once the entitlement of kings and queens.

Each villa has a *huge* bathroom which features a large bath; a vast, open shower area; and "his and hers" vanity basins, spaced well apart. A blind, located between the basins, can be lifted to open the room to the bedroom and the lagoon view beyond. The main window behind the shower area is frosted as it faces the pontoon leading to other villas. In an alcove on one side there's hanging space and ironing facilities to posh up for evenings at restaurants.

The large bedroom has a European feeling of opulence, with lots of rich, dark wood and lavish, curtain fabric which cossets guests by providing them with a completely dark room for sleeping. The large living-room has a table and chairs plus long couches which are covered with bursts of bright tropical color.

If you want to impress your special someone, the size of the rooms and the classical European fittings give a prestigious "look" which now can only be found at this resort. (The old Hilton Nui had this classical décor and under the Conrad flag has been completely refurbished with a fresh, artful, modern look.

If you're seeking a couple's haven, you're likely to be wanting lots of time in your bungalow. To get a nice view at St Regis you *must* pay for an overwater bungalow with a *mountain view* as the other over-water bungalows look back, across a section of the lagoon, to the palm covered motu where the local neighbors live.

Another good choice would be to book an on-land villa. These have their own pool and plenty of private space around them. The ones on the reef side are most secluded and the only sound you're likely to hear will be the splash of waves on the reef. We fell in love with the beach villas on our first visit to St Regis. Along with the extra space and the pool, they also have a mountain view from their private, white-sand beach. They're the most affordable way to have a pool, they're very spacious, and cost less than staying overwater. There are only a few of each so you will have to book early to secure one of these.

A plus that many couples appreciate about St Regis is that it's the only resort around the island with a dedicated couple's pool. The artistic design of the Oasis pool, with lots of private nooks for canoodling, is very lovely. You'll probably have the whole area to yourselves as so many couples loll around their overwater bungalow when not out on excursion. We last stayed in peak season and noticed that there was rarely anyone there.

Intercontinental Thalasso

The Intercontinental Thalasso feels like it has been designed for couples. You're unlikely to meet a child staying there as it's all overwater bungalows and doesn't offer any bonuses for kids. The overwater bungalows have a modern, airy décor and their luxurious 1000 square feet provides the perfect size and comforts for two people to enjoy "togetherness". They are closer together on the piers than some other resorts which could reduce quietness and privacy, depending on who stays next door.

We think of the Thalasso as a 4-and-a-half- star resort as we have found the level of service and quality of food is far superior to 4-star Bora Bora resorts. The Thalasso costs much less than Four seasons and St Regis and it's really worth stepping up and paying a little more than a 4-star hotel; especially if it's your honeymoon or anniversary. All the Bora Bora 4-star and 5-star hotels include breakfast for a great rate and Thalasso offers an attractive rate to add in three course gourmet dinners. The French influence is huge and we really enjoyed both the food and attentive service, in the delightful island surrounds.

The Thalasso has a focus on eco-tourism, offering salt water air conditioning and photo-voltaic cell power. Another feature of this resort is the high-tech Deep Ocean Spa which covers a large area of the grounds and offers many experiences that are usually only found in Europe. If you book any spa treatment, you are entitled to the use of the facilities for an entire afternoon. We highly recommend doing this as we felt brand new at the end of the day!

Those desiring a large, super-luxurious pad can book one of the newly built 2-story villas which have been given the glamorous Brando name. A couple could play in one of these all week without having to leave their "room".

FOR A FAMILY VACATION

Although Bora Bora is usually depicted as a couples' destination, families can have an exceptional vacation on this island, too. There are various factors to consider when choosing family accommodation and their importance will vary according to the age and number of children.

- Are your children at an age where you will be able to relax in an overwater bungalow? If not, choose a resort with spacious garden or beach bungalows. These thatched-roof on-land villas give an extraordinary island style vacation too.
- Do you want to pay for an extra bedroom? If not, choose a bungalow with a separate living room – you can even leave extra beds made up in the daytime. It's good use of space as you may never sit in the living room. With the warm temperatures and beautiful views, the deck is likely to be your favorite living area.
- What outdoor complimentary activities does the resort offer for the family to enjoy together?

- Do you want to enjoy quality couple's time together without being "mum" and "dad"? Choose a resort that offers a complimentary kid's club which is available on any day that you wish to use this amazing resource. The kids will probably have even more fun that you!

The top family-friendly resorts in Bora Bora are Four Seasons, Conrad Nui and St Regis. For a moderate priced hotel, Le Meridien is a good choice. Read the chapter on *Family Friendly Bora Bora* to find out why these hotels are the best for those with children.

TO SEE THE SUNSET OR SUNRISE

Bora Bora has stunning sunsets. Even on evenings when the enormous sky is not ablaze with a myriad of oranges and pinks, observing the huge golden orb drop slowly into the ocean is an extraordinary event. If you want to experience these inspiring moments, it could influence where you stay.

Watching the sun rise in Bora Bora is special too. I know that some of you will be horrified by talk of getting up for sunrise. Back home you're a night owl, like me, and you think a vacation is for sleeping in! But in the ion-rich air of this tiny, Pacific island you're likely to feel yourself pleasurably relaxed and sinking into the comfort of your bungalow bed earlier than expected. That's great, because Bora Bora is awesome in the early morning; you won't want to sleep it away. To see and feel all that's best about Bora Bora, plan to be up for a sunrise – even if you view it from your luxurious bath at Four Seasons. Each day dawns with a fresh newness and the lagoon gleams translucent with a stillness that is only present at the beginning of day. It's worth getting up for ... and so are the breakfast buffets!

These resorts have the best sunset views:

Conrad Bora Bora Nui

Conrad Nui is the only resort which faces the reef and western horizon. This means that Nui has wonderful all-year-round panoramic views of the sun setting *into* the water. These can be seen from the large hillside restaurant, the new overwater bar, and most of villas. The 2 Presidential Villas, which are at the very end of the longest pontoon, have the most incredible sunset panorama on the island. If you can splurge on a Presidential Villa, you'll make sunset memories beyond your dreams. We had the good fortune to stay in one of these so Melinda and Tom posed on the edge of the overwater swimming pool for some playful, silhouette shots. Tom had popped the big question over a candle-lit dinner on the beach. Months later, one of these awesome photos became the background image on their wedding "Save the Date" notification for relatives and friends to stick on their fridge.

Four Seasons Bora Bora

Four Seasons has the most northerly position of the resorts located on the eastern coral ring of motus. During winter, when the sun is moving in a more northerly path across the sky, we noticed that; from the beach and the Sunset Bar; we could see the sun sinking into the water to the north of the main island.

Apart from that narrow winter window; the sun sets behind Bora Bora's main island when viewed from Four Seasons, St Regis, Le Meridien, the Intercontinental Thalasso and the Sofitel Private Island. That creates special moments too. Watching the sun set behind majestic Mt Otemanu is also spectacular! The famous signature peak becomes a dramatic silhouette lit up by a golden, pink or orange sky.

These resorts have the best sunrise views:

St Regis Resort

The St Regis Reef Villas face east across the Pacific Ocean so are fantastic for fans of sunrise. Staying in one of these you'll also hear waves splashing onto the rocks of the coral reef sheltering the lagoon. These on-land villas have private pools and they're in a secluded part of the resort, quite a distance from the restaurants. We like this location because we enjoy riding our bicycles through the lovely resort grounds around curved paths which are lit up by lovely coral-stone lanterns in the evening.

The St Regis has also taken advantage of this eastern aspect by locating a yoga platform to capture a wide view of the rising sun.

Intercontinental Thalasso

The Intercontinental Thalasso has an interesting track leading across to the ocean side of the resort. Early morning risers can exercise (and wear off their dinner) while watching the sun rise over the ocean, before heading to the wonderful (not to be missed) international breakfast buffet that Thalasso graciously serves up with an impressive flair.

5 STAR LUXURY

Deciding "Which resort is best?"

Four Seasons v St Regis

"Which resort is best?" For years this has been a hot topic on internet forums focused on Bora Bora. It's the question we are most frequently asked by site visitors, who are struggling to make the most important decision while planning an extraordinary wedding or honeymoon. There's been a dilemma in choosing between the St Regis and the Four Seasons, which happen to be located in the same area of the world's most admired lagoon.

We were curious too. We'd been seeing gorgeous photographs of the last resort to be constructed in Bora Bora and thinking that we would save it for a special occasion. On a recent trip we took along my partner Tom. He'd been to Tahiti several times but I had the pleasure of introducing him to my passion, Bora Bora. A lawyer by trade, he's a romantic guy who knows how to appreciate the finest things that life has to offer and seriously loves water sports. This was a great opportunity to vacation at both resorts, back-to-back, in overwater bungalows of similar pricing. This enabled us to do a direct comparison of these 2 luxury resorts, during the most popular season of the year.

We'd loved *everything* about St Regis when we were last there in a quiet time of the year. By staying at both, on the same vacation, we expected to find which resort was number one. But what we discovered is that there is *no clear-cut winner* as each offers a completely different experience.

I'll share one little personal aside. Tom's favorite was actually the Four Seasons, but he was completely swept away during our private lagoon-side dinner at St Regis and asked me to be his wife. He didn't even have a ring to slip onto my finger!

After our nights at Four Seasons and St Regis we had an even bigger surprise. The newly re-opened luxury resort, on the opposite side of the lagoon - which we stayed at after the St Regis and Four Seasons - was so spectacular that we found there's a new question. Read on to find out why.

Scenery and setting

We began our vacation, in mid-June, at the Four Seasons. As this was our first time at Four Seasons our travel agent warned us that we were starting with the best. (She believes in saving the best till last, which is why she recommends that if you plan to see a few isles in Tahiti, you finish your vacation on Bora Bora.) On arrival we realized why she had said that. We were speechless as we were whizzed through the grounds of Four Seasons and were amazed that the last to be built resort has incomparable scenic beauty, even though it is further from Mt Otemano than other eastern resorts. It has the most dramatic of *all* resort views across to iconic Mt Otemanu from *all around the resort*. Although the St Regis is situated close to the Four Seasons, the sandy, coral motus that the two resorts are set out on are quite different and provide a very different outlook for the guests staying at each resort.

St Regis also offers a world class vacation but you *must book a Mountain View bungalow* or you could spend your whole holiday hardly seeing Bora Bora's signature peak - apart from when you arrive at, and depart from, the boat dock; or visit the spa. We had a bungalow in a long row, facing back towards the palm fringed motu where neighboring islander's live. The only times we saw the mountain view were when we rode our bicycles (which were loads of fun to get around on) and had glimpses between the bungalows of more fortunate guests, on the other side of the pontoon, who had Mountain View villas. When we visited the spa, we had a view of the tip of the mountain from the reception area and the spa beach, where we enjoyed a private romantic dinner.

From the main areas of the resort; including breakfast, lunch and dinner venues, the pool and the beach; guests look out to a corner of the lagoon with a backdrop of the palm fringed motu.

Lagoon, the renowned overwater restaurant with Chef Jean-Georges Vongerichten's cuisine, is situated alongside the boat dock and offers the best views to be found anywhere around the resort. Sipping drinks at the gleaming bar or dining out on the deck at sunset, with the Mt Otemanu view, is an exceptional experience. We enjoyed this on our previous visit, during summer, when the daylight hours are longer. This time, on the first night we had booked they moved dining inside for fear of rain. It was "winter" in Bora Bora, so darkness fell before we were seated at our table and we were looking at room reflections on the dark glass wall. Unluckily, we cancelled a third night and the sky turned on a spectacular pink and orange sunset. As we rode past Lagoon, to get to the dock and view it, we observed diners being shown to their tables on the deck.

This resort has lovely features and amenities and you can enjoy all that's best about Bora Bora by opting for a Mountain View bungalow. Make sure you book early to secure one.

At Four Seasons we were reminded that we were in Bora Bora every moment of our stay. The signature black-rock mountain is an icon for us. From our breakfast table we could see Mt Otemanu between the soaring palm trees. Walking to and from the bungalows we were astonished by wonderful views the entire way along the paths and over the bridges and down the pontoon. Everywhere we walked around this resort we were dawdling to savor and snap the views. It was a fantasy that had come to life. Most guests even get a Mt Otemanu view without booking a Mountain View category as most bungalows get a view to part of the mountain from one end of their balcony. From the beach, the pool, the spa, the bungalows, and dining venues; you see Bora Bora's main island, with Mt Otemanu's basalt rocks towering over it, as a panoramic backdrop!

These two resorts may be in a similar location but the aspect, and ambiance at the St Regis and Four Seasons are quite different. Read our detailed commentary, comparing important aspects of these two resorts, and decide which one will provide *you* with the best Bora Bora vacation.

Bungalows

A huge part of a Bora Bora resort stay is the novelty of having a thatched-roof bungalow. If you choose well it will be an extra pleasurable stay and you're likely to spend lots of time enjoying it. The location, aspect, interior design, and condition of your bungalow is important. Here's what we experienced in similar priced overwater bungalows at these top resorts:

Four Seasons

- Four Seasons overwater villas are the most recently built in Bora Bora, and it shows. Their positioning on pontoons and brilliant design maximizes the views whilst also giving a high level of privacy. These bungalows have much more space between them than those at St Regis (or other resorts in Bora Bora) and they're angled so that you can't see your neighbors and they can't see you – even when you sit on your deck or jump into the water from your private pontoon.
- The 1000 square feet size of our overwater bungalow gave us the perfect amount of gracious space to have a feeling of intimacy and know we were *over the Bora Bora lagoon* in a hut; which was exactly what we had come for.

- On stepping into our villa, we were seduced at first sight; it felt so luxurious and spacious, and had expansive views. The perfect layout ensures that every room has a superb window to the lagoon.
- The elegant interior-design and classical furnishings feature light teak-wood and Polynesian artwork. Each room has timber shutters, replacing the usual curtains, and they slide open to show off the thrilling views. We slept with shutters wide open and awoke to a brilliant blue.
- The bathroom's oversized tub has shutters to slide the whole "wall" open and reveal turquoise water. We began the morning with a soak in the tub – out of sight – while marveling at the beauty of the lagoon.
- The bedroom spoke of romance. Alongside the bed there's a lover's nook with a side window to the lagoon. I truly felt like I was sleeping over the water and waking up in the luxurious bed, overlooking the lagoon, was a dream come true.
- The villa's deck was a perfect size for maximizing outdoor time and the proportions enabled us to also feel close to the lagoon from inside the villa. One side of the deck has sun-lounges and there's a shady, thatched-roof covered dining area on the other. We enjoyed ordering room service to linger over lunch on the outside deck. It's the ultimate water-view, private dining.
- You can choose to book a bungalow with a pool on the deck. This is a wonderful add-on amenity if you enjoy swimming pools. The lagoon water below the bungalow was appealing to us and were very happy to jump in there.
- The bungalow decks have a lower pontoon area which you can jump from, sunbake on, and access the ladder to the lagoon.
- Glass floor-panels showcase the turquoise lagoon and let in light.
- The same current that sweeps past the St Regis bungalows flows past the Four Seasons bungalows but the water at the Four Seasons was clearer than the St Regis water.
- The Four Seasons bungalows are spread out between two main arms, that both divide into two towards the end. This means that the "rooms" are spread out over a vast area, most of which you don't ever see. When you go to and from your bungalow you feel like you are one of the lucky few basking in island paradise.
- There's a separate track alongside the lagoon for walkers to get to their pontoons; and a completely private track to the awesome on-land villas, which each have their own private beach (out-of-reach to others). We felt like celebs staying in one of these!

29

- The walk to our bungalow was quite far as we were on the second arm of bungalows which head out from the beach. Although there were no bikes, it was do-able and strolling around was delightful. The lush grounds are an exotic paradise with interesting pathways and charming wooden bridges to cross the streams which lead to inner lagoons. We stopped frequently along the way to capture special moments on camera.

St Regis

- The St Regis over water bungalows are the largest in Bora Bora, starting at 1500 square feet. We certainly noticed that ours was huge and the size and the classical European furnishings gave a feeling of grandeur. The living area is so spacious that you can sleep an extra person without impacting day-time use of the room.
- The shape of the deck made the distance to the lagoon water further. The view, from the bed to the water, was obstructed by the rectangular deck being positioned outwards so we were looking over the sun-lounges and through a thatched roof area with an outdoor table setting.
- The curtains block out all light when closed. This gives those who prefer to sleep in the dark a good night's rest.
- The bathroom is huge. It's one large space which includes the wardrobe area. It's located behind the bedroom so you must walk through the bedroom to access it. There's a long, deep, oblong tub but it didn't have the appeal of the Four Seasons bath-with-a-view so on our 5-night stay it went unused.
- To get to the toilet cubicle, guests must go through the bathroom which has a completely open shower, a bath, and basin area. This limits privacy, especially if you have an extra person.
- The water under the St Regis bungalows is turquoise but cloudy. It's not as clear in this part of the lagoon so the water around the bungalow was less desirable to swim in. But we did have great fun jumping from our deck and swimming across to the ladder to get back up. As there's no coral under these bungalows we saw little marine life.
- There was quite a strong current sweeping from the motu at the back of the resort towards the main island across the other side of the lagoon. This meant it was impossible to use the inflatable floaties that we had taken for having fun in the lagoon.
- The distance from the main area of the resort to our bungalow was too far to walk, especially in the hot weather. It was even further to the spa. We

used bikes whenever there were some available and this made the journey fun. Bikes were in demand and there was a shortage.

- Most guests must use the same path to get to their bungalows, making it a busy thoroughfare of bikes, walkers and golf buggies. Even folk staying in some of the top villas have this traffic passing by.
- At the St Regis we heard bouts of jet-ski noise outside our bungalow. We were also affected by our neighboring guests on each side, either from noise or from them watching us while on our outdoor deck or in the water.

Beach

The Four Seasons

- *A picture paints a thousand words* so go to our playful site-page about the Four Seasons beach and see it for yourself. We wriggled our toes in pure white sand, mesmerized by the turquoise water with a dramatic panorama of the mountain behind. The overwater bungalows, in the foreground on one side, add to the romance; and on the other side, just meters from shore, there's a tiny sandy isle which you can wade to, with your honey. The sensational *panoramic "wow" factor and decadent service* on the Four Seasons beach made being there an unforgettable experience.
- French-blue umbrellas sit alongside lagoon, providing shade on the plush sun beds – which are promptly covered with fitted towels; upon the arrival of guests.
- A row of large thatched-roof umbrellas gives complete shade – plus prime, front row views of Mt Otemanu.
- The service on the beach was extraordinary, right to the water's edge. Bar drinks, never-ending complimentary iced water, and the interesting menu available at the lunch restaurants could be enjoyed over most of the day.
- There are broken pieces of coral in the water, so we needed to wear reef shoes for swimming.

St Regis

- The St Regis beach does not compete with the stunning resort beaches that are discussed earlier in the book. It does offer a long stretch of white-sand, with calm, shallow water. But if you've sunned on some of the others, the outlook is disappointing. When I waded out into the water, and looked to the left, I could catch a glimpse of the mountain.

- If you're coming to hang out in your overwater bungalow, and not particularly a beach type, this will not detract from your vacation. You can enjoy the lagoon water *and* have an awesome mountain view, simply by choosing a villa in that category.
- The most romantic sights are a hammock-for-two that's standing in the water at the far end of the beach, and a thatched roof shelter-for-two overlooking the beach. They both provide a perfect location to linger and watch the sunset.
- Like most of Tahiti, there are pieces of broken coral in the water of this beach, so it's preferable to swim with reef shoes here too.

Pool

Four Seasons

- The large wave-shaped Four Seasons pool, nestled between soaring palm trees, is situated behind the main beach area with a direct panorama across the lagoon to Mt Otemanu.
- A row of glamorous, pool cabanas provide more shade and privacy than those at the other resorts that have them.
- The bar is located on one side of the pool area, but the wait staff are so attentive that you won't need to get up to order, unless you want to.

St Regis

- The main pool area is behind the beach at St Regis, partly separated from the beach by the bar. There are no dramatic views across to Bora Bora's main island and signature peak from here. Looking from the pool area, in the opposite direction to the bar and beach, I could just see the very tip of the mountain, except for the times of day when it was obscured by the clouds floating past it.
- At one end the pool offers a convenient swim-up bar with stools and on the side offers comfy, low loungers that are half in, half out of, the water.
- This rectangular, main St Regis pool appears smaller than the one at Four Seasons and had more people in it, and around it, as the beach lacks the appeal of the one at Four Seasons. Plus, more bungalows at Four Seasons

have their own pool and/or private beach, making the main beach there even more special for hanging out.

- The second pool, a romantic, adult's-only pool, Oasis, offers a plus to couples who are seeking quiet romance. Oasis has private cabanas, placed in different areas around the pool. It's in a secluded setting, surrounded by trees. While lounging poolside here, snack deliveries can be ordered from the private dining menu and are delivered by cart.

Spa

Four Seasons

The beautiful Four Seasons spa is set on the ocean side of the motu and designed to capture dramatic views from both the front and the back. The reef side looks over the rugged, royal-blue ocean. The side facing the lagoon has sublime views of turquoise water, backed by soaring palm trees, with Mt Otemanu reaching sky-wards in the distance. The spa building has high cathedral ceilings that add to an *out of this world* feeling.

Spa treatments are provided indoors or in outdoor pavilions among the palm trees. One large treatment room has the Mt Otemanu view plus glass flooring to show off the lagoon. This luxurious room offers couples an ultimate romantic experience.

Ladies at Four Seasons have an extra-special treat. Their private plunge-pool area has a vision of turquoise water and soaring palm trees with majestic Mt Otemanu framed right in the center. Gentleman have the reef view to the Pacific Ocean. At one time in the evenings, men may join their ladies and enjoy the perfectly framed view together.

St Regis

The St Regis Spa also has a quiet location, on a small motu, with the lagoonarium circling around it. It's in a world of its own. Apart from the view to Mt Otemanu from the boat dock, the spa reception area has the most beautiful view to be found around the communal grounds of this resort. The secluded spa beach makes a striking background for photographs, or a picturesque foreground while having a private dinner in the evening.

At St Regis, there are no spa rooms offering glass-floor lagoon views or water views outside their windows. After leaving the open reception area, which has the view, you are inside white walls and could be anywhere in the world while having a treatment. After being pampered, guests are taken to an air-conditioned relaxation room which also has the lovely view of the spa beach with the top of Mt Otemanu showing in the backdrop. The ladies' facilities; including a sauna, steam room and outdoor plunge pool; have a white coral-stone wall bordering a courtyard that features bright pink flowers and has a Mediterranean feel.

Food

Four Seasons

- We were pleased with the wide variety of tasty food that was so easily available – all around the resort - throughout the day and enjoyed sensational views while eating breakfast, lunch, and dinner.
- The breakfast buffet was a superbly presented feast. The excellent selection of island-fare included fresh drinking coconuts and nicely prepared, juicy, tropical fruit. The platters on the display were replaced in a timely way as they emptied. The dishes prepared on request from the kitchen looked very tempting when they arrived on the table.
- We enjoyed every meal we ordered from Fare Hoa, including the luxury of having some lunches served on our deck and the beach. Even the salads were a treat as they were imbued with French flair. Prices were reasonable for a top resort on a distant isle.
- The Sunset Bar is a lovely evening "venue with a view" for enjoying fresh, tasty sushi and cocktails as the sun sets behind the mountain.

St Regis

- The St Regis breakfast buffet offered a wide selection of international food choices. There was something to please everyone, but it wasn't as well laid out as at Four Seasons. The fruit selection was cut into large chunks and a powerful juicer was provided at each side for guests to create fresh fruit juices of their favored combinations. We ate overlooking the beach.
- The Aparima Bar has a very long menu for casual eating at lunch or dinner. It included many tempting Asian dishes and we discovered that the main chef was Asian which would also explain why the dishes at Bam Boo were so good. The salads were extremely simple, yet the vegetables didn't appear very fresh.

- We'd been very impressed with Lagoon, the French fine-dining restaurant, on our previous visit to St Regis. The gleaming restaurant and bar hovers over water facing the very best view that can be found anywhere around this resort. Sadly, we missed out on the Mt Otemanu view during our stay. On one of our nights they had moved dining inside for fear of rain and, on another, it was already dark when we arrived so we couldn't see a view out of the glass wall of windows because of the reflections inside. (Regretfully, we cancelled another booking as that night Bora Bora turned on a most glorious sunset.) At Lagoon the food was very artistically arranged on the plate and our dishes were tasty but the size of each serve was quite small. Lagoon is a good choice for a special celebration and you can arrange to go there from other resorts. But you must understand that although you will be served with great attention to detail, you cannot order the weather! It's an enclosed building with air-conditioning so, if you feel the cold, do take something to throw over once you step inside.
- One evening, we tried a variety of dishes at Far Niente, the Italian restaurant, but we are serious foodies and didn't find any of them memorable.
- The winning restaurant at St Regis was the Japanese nook which has been given a new look and reopened as Bam Boo. We ate there several times and everything we ordered looked fresh and tasted delicious. Each dish that arrived on our table was a colorful, decorative feast.

St Regis Butler Service

St Regis takes great pride in the butler service. It's the only resort in Bora Bora where this service is offered to all guests. In practice, these butlers are special concierges, with more personality and training.

After registering at reception on arrival, we were greeted by Sebastian, the butler who was assigned to assist us throughout our stay. He was friendly and knowledgeable and for the most part it felt like he was *our* butler. Much to our shock we saw him being equally friendly and helpful to strangers at breakfast and other groups of people during the day. We had to come to terms with the fact that he was many other people's butler too!

Sebastian would appear, like a genie, and ask us which restaurant we wished to dine at. He forgot to make our booking for the Italian restaurant and when we showed up there was initial consternation, but the wait staff quickly organized a table outside.

Calling the butler desk from the phone puts you in touch with an in-house team of butlers who, it is said, can organize anything you may need – clothes ironed, coffee delivered, or a dinner pick-up. These invisible on-call butlers are different from the smartly dressed ones with a profile, who interact with guests on a face to face basis.

One morning, a butler from Italy picked us up as we were walking to the marine biologist's talk. He was courteous, with a charming personality, and within a few minutes I had fallen in love! The butler service is a useful convenience that can handle both frivolous and practical requests, just from a call. But what sets this service apart – from guest services at other resorts – is the personality of your assigned butler and the relationship that develops between you and him. After a few days your butler can feel like an old friend and you may wonder how other resorts work without this cosseting.

One evening we had an unexpected medical emergency at dinner. The feeling of being far from home, and on a small island, was eased when Sebastian arrived a few minutes after we had asked a waiter to phone for him. It was easy to tell him in English what was wrong, and he immediately rang for an on-call doctor (working for the clinic on the main island) to come to the resort. He brought the doctor to our bungalow an hour later. At the end of the visit the doctor insisted on being paid $400 in cash, which we weren't carrying. Sebastian broke the awkward silence by stating that he would organize for the resort to pay the fee and charge it to our account. We may have had this assistance at any resort but the familiarity and trust that we had built up with Sebastian made me feel more secure.

Summing Up

St Regis incorporates a feeling of a prestigious, European atmosphere with pristine, tropical island surrounds. Guests can stay in spacious grandeur, with a choice of levels of privacy, while visiting the sensational natural beauty of the world's most admired lagoon. They can enjoy a variety of activities and luxurious indulgences.

Four Seasons has brilliantly maximized its location on a motu facing the world's most beautiful island. This magical resort offers picture-perfect, exotic grounds with popular activities; an extraordinary panorama of Bora Bora's main island from all around the resort; and romantic overwater villas. There's a myriad of visual treats that can't be found anywhere else on the planet.

TIPS FOR STAYING AT ST REGIS

- If you want a quiet room, avoid what we now refer to as "Jet-ski Alley!" The area between the St Regis overwater bungalows and the beach that's across the water is used by tour providers leading groups of jet-skiers and other noisy water craft. We realized this while taking a jet-ski tour around the island from Matira Beach. Suddenly we understood what most of the traffic noise, that we'd heard from our St Regis overwater bungalow, was. If you don't want to feel like you're at Sea-world, and you do want to see that you're in Bora Bora, then choose another villa category. This row of bungalows can also be subjected to smoke blowing from the neighbors burning depot. Noise and smoke are definite avoids on your vacation of a lifetime!

- **Pay for a Mount Otemanu view** or you may only see the majestic mountain view when you arrive and leave the resort. Those who want to spend less on accommodation will find value and fun in a beach or reef villa with a pool, which is what we booked the first time. Choose well and you will have a fabulous Stay at St Regis. But if you don't use these first 2 tips on accommodation, don't say we didn't warn you!

- **Email ahead of time and book an outdoor table at Lagoon, alongside the water.** Choose an evening early in your stay as you may have an exceptional experience and want to go again. Book for the time they open, to enjoy drinks at the bar and watch the sun set over Mt Otemanu. We had some extraordinary sunsets and the only way to view them is at Lagoon or booking a bungalow with a mountain view.

- **Book a private dinner on the spa beach.** Organize this well ahead of going to be sure of an available night. The intimate dinner for 2 is served on two beaches but the spa beach has the special aspect. Our dinner for two was the best meal we ate at this Resort.

- **Talk to a specialist travel agent if you're going for a honeymoon or anniversary.** You're likely to get bonuses such as a couple's massage, romantic flower-bed, champagne, and pastries on arrival.

- **Bring footwear and clothing that will feel comfortable while riding a bike.** You can wear a skirt, you just need to be able to hitch it up over your knees. Don't worry if you haven't ridden a bike for decades. The lovely paths are safe and such fun to ride around. We rode to breakfast, lunch, and dinner, the spa, the pool, and the beach. You may come out from dinner and find that the pool boys have collected up all the bicycles which were left in the main area of the resort. This is the time to send for a buggy.

- If you are visiting St Regis after a stay at Le Meridien (both Starwoods), you can request that a boat pick you up to transfer you directly instead of going back to the airport for a pick-up. This saves time and money.

A vacation in Bora Bora should be the vacation of a lifetime! We left the Four Seasons wanting more, wishing we could stay longer, and talking about revisiting next time. But we left the St Regis feeling quite disappointed that we hadn't been aware of the awesome benefits of booking a Mountain View bungalow.

TIPS FOR STAYING AT FOUR SEASONS

- Book a Mountain View room category to have front row seats to the enchanting Mount Otemanu aspect. But if you can't step up to this level, many of the Lagoon View over water bungalows at the Four Seasons have a view to Mt Otemanu from their deck. You may not have the mountain directly in front of you, but you can see it from one end of your deck and enjoy the whole panorama while you walk to your bungalow.
- If you wish to float off your bungalow, ask to be in one facing west. The water flows west and if you're tied to the east side of the pontoon you will be floating *under* the bungalows! We were unable to use our floaties because our bungalow was on the east side of the pontoon.
- To have the maximum amount of sunshine on your deck, ask for a west facing bungalow. These bungalows will get the afternoon sun and will also give a sunset view each evening.
- If you want privacy, avoid the bungalows on the east side that are next to the main dock. Excursion providers and shuttle boats frequently pass these bungalows.
- Order room service and linger over eating on your luxurious deck. It's the best waterside dining experience you will have without paying the price for a private dinner by the lagoon.
- If you'd like to dine outside of the resort one night, organize a transfer to the St Regis to try out the cuisine at Lagoon restaurant. Book ahead of time and request a table outside by the water.
- Four Seasons does not have bikes so, to get around, you will need to either stroll or be shuttled in a buggy. The resort and bungalows are spread out over large distances. Bring shoes that are comfortable to walk in. At busy

times you may wait an hour for a buggy to pick you up. Be prepared to walk. We took great pleasure in walking hand in hand through the tropical gardens and it certainly helped with our step count each day!

- If you have limited mobility, let the resort know at the time of booking so they can assign you a bungalow that is closest to the facilities. A Beach View category bungalow or on-land villa will be the best room categories for you.
- Be aware that this is the hardest resort to leave as is has the least frequent shuttle times and charges the most for the shuttle. This may or may not be an issue for you. The resort was so beautiful that we didn't want to ever, ever, leave! The resort grounds abound with many activities and you can also book a variety of tours that will pick you up from the resort dock. It will only be a problem if you want to try different restaurants and shop at the local markets. Then this may not be the resort for you.

Fortunately, there's now another exciting choice for staying in luxury, out on a motu, while also having easy access to the main island. If you want your bungalow to be in mint condition, check out (and check into) the new 5-star that's shining in Bora Bora!

A NEW CONTENDER FOR *BEST RESORT*

Yes, the topic of *"which resort is best"* has become even more intriguing. You're about to discover that there's more choice for an extraordinary honeymoon or vacation in Bora Bora. In fact, you can now have the honeymoon of your dreams for less money than you would pay at either the Four Seasons or St Regis!

After our 5 nights at St Regis we moved to the beautiful Bora Bora Nui. Previously, known as the "Hilton Bora Bora Nui", this resort closed for a complete revamp before re-opening, in March 2017, under the prestigious Conrad brand. We took the St Regis shuttle-boat to the airport and Conrad's 2 story airport shuttle-boat to Nui. From the moment we stepped onto the dock and saw the dazzling, new overwater bar we knew we had arrived somewhere special.

We were thrilled to discover that Conrad is the new star shining in Bora Bora. After the transformation everything gleams and sparkles. Yet this impressive, world-class resort retains the true tropical isle experience that has always wowed visitors to this lush, volcanic motu. The quality and creativity of the revamp makes the Nui a top contender for "Best Resort in Bora Bora"!

In the past, Nui was popular with those wanting romantic, peaceful seclusion as it's tucked away in a quiet area of the lagoon, far from the noise of the boats that transport people and goods around the more trafficked parts of the island. This resort doesn't have a direct mountain view (except from several overwater bungalows) but, *what it does have,* more than makes up for this.

The Conrad Nui offers superb luxury with a natural, eye-pleasing flair. The layout and design compliment the extraordinary beauty of its exotic setting. The owner takes a personal interest in Nui and has put her impeccable taste into action - in both the interior decorating and the grounds - resulting in a seamless, flawless presentation.

Every item of utility around the hotel also enhances the ambient beauty of the island. For example; the chairs blend harmoniously into the landscape and are as lovely to look at as they are to sit on.

Aspect & Views

The island aspect from the villas and main areas of Nui is completely different to the outlook at Four Seasons, St Regis, and the other resorts on the eastern coral ring of motus. Only several Nui villas offer Mt Otemanu views. Instead, the main areas of the resort and the villas have wide, watery – all the way to the horizon – glistening vistas that inspire a deep sense of tranquility.

Immaculate bungalows in a Choice of Locations

The size and layout of the overwater villas provides a perfect intimate space for a honeymoon or romantic vacation. Some have the extra luxury of a pool on the deck. These villas are set over the bluest water in Bora Bora and have *abundant, living coral underneath for snorkeling straight from your bungalow.*

There's also a selection of bungalows/villas on land, in a choice of locations. Two superb beach villas have been newly constructed just a few steps from the sand and one of the most entertaining snorkeling spots in Bora Bora. Nui's beach is so long that you'll usually have the area to yourself.

All the bungalows have been refurbished to a very high standard and are impeccably clean, classy and luxurious. Some of those on land provide a little more space and/or have a private pool. The wardrobe area in the bungalows is the best I have seen for ease in accessing your belongings without having to see clutter. Unlike some other Bora Bora resorts, *every* "room" at Conrad is a good one, and in a serene location. You're not taking a gamble when you book a vacation here.

Do you want the luxury and prestige of staying in one of the very best overwater bungalows in Bora Bora?

The two glamorous Conrad Presidential villas are double-story overwater palaces in a very private location at the end of a pier. They've been a talking point for years and many rich and famous folk have vacationed in them. They offer extraordinary space, amenities and service; plus, their incredible outlook has the best sunset views on the island. The only other overwater bungalows that can be compared to the Presidential villas are the new split-level Brando villas a the Intercontinental Thalasso.

Eating at Conrad

Eating leisurely, surrounded by entrancing views, was a very pleasurable part of our Conrad stay. We enjoyed a wide variety of graciously served, good quality meals at several restaurants.

Feasting at the not-to-be-missed international breakfast buffet was an idyllic way to begin the day; lunching casually at the feet-in-the-sand beach restaurant or in a watery niche near the pool bar was blissful; and in the evenings, we rotated between the high-up-with-views-to-the-horizon Iriatai; the Chinese restaurant, which is alongside a waterfall; and nibbling over drinks at the zany Upa Upa Bar, which has the very best sunset view in Bora Bora. The fun memories are indelible in my mind.

Pool

If you have fantasized about lazing at the waterside, cocktail in hand, in perfect temperatures, on a tropical island; Conrad Nui has the best pool in Bora Bora to bring your day-dreams to life! Conrad's pool has so many gorgeous niches to hang-out in that it surpassed even my imagination! Make sure you book enough nights to enjoy everything about this awesome resort.

Beach

Beach-lovers will be interested to hear that the Conrad is the only top Bora Bora resort with a *natural* beach. We've featured Conrad's beach in our 2018 calendar; it's the longest and most secluded resort beach in Bora Bora and the scenery *under* the water is fantastic too. We discovered that Nui has some of the most amazing snorkeling in Bora Bora, just a few meters from the beach. It's also the best resort beach for enjoying a variety of complimentary water activities. Long after returning home I was reminiscing about perfect (winter) days on the Conrad beach.

Bars

Relaxation is an artform at Conrad and the two new awesome bars continue the theme. One is the pool bar, mentioned above, and the other is the Upa Upa Bar which now has the prime overwater position that reception had in the Hilton era. On our previous vacation, we stood with our backs to the horizon while registering and departing! This visit we sat back, with tropical drinks and nibbles in hand, marveling at the golden-orbed sun sinking into the mirror-like ocean.

There's never a crowd around the Conrad bars. They're romantic places to make memories while enjoying each other, the music and the gorgeous surrounds. Even non-drinkers can linger to watch the sunset as the menu includes fruity no-alcohol Tahiti cocktails and tasty snacks. The knowledgeable bar staff offer just the right balance of professionalism and friendliness to create a convivial atmosphere like we enjoyed at Four Seasons. Perhaps it's because both resorts have a focus on employing locals.

Getting Around the Resort

Getting around the grounds of the Conrad was part of the fun. The Conrad grounds are large (but not as large as Four Seasons and St Regis) so guests can call for a lift. Golf cars are great for rainy weather or if you get all dressed up for dinner. (One night we were given a ride after dining and an islander worker sat at the back of the cart serenading us all the way to our villa. There are so many out-of-our-usual-world surprises in Tahiti.) At other times riding around, in the island air on a bike, gives a sense of freedom. It was even more fun at the Conrad than St Regis as the new bikes were in perfect condition. It's pink for girls and blue for the boys to easily identify the two different sizes. Although you can choose to have a villa in closer proximity to the restaurants, we loved being at the very end of a pontoon on one side of the grounds. We recommend that anyone who is able-bodied pack clothing (including skirts) that will enable them to ride. Your vacation will be extra thrilling.

Hill-top Spa

Set high on the hill, amongst ancient volcanic rocks, the unique Conrad spa resonates with an almost religious ambiance. The area has magnificent views over the top of the resort, across the blue lagoon, and all the way to the distant horizon. It's a totally different view to that of Four Seasons spa, yet just as remarkable. Each treatment room is in a little thatched villa, perched amongst awe-inspiring, black lava rocks. There's a natural simplicity which contrasts with the elegant sophistication at Four Seasons spa. Nui also offers a luxurious, Polynesian nurturing for couples.

Every aspect of the Conrad Resort maximizes the magical beauty that makes Bora Bora legendary. During our stay I was infused by a deep calm and came home refreshed; certain that *life is for enjoying!*

So how do you choose between the top 3 resorts?

To have the most luxurious Bora Bora vacation, we recommend comparing what the Four Seasons, the St Regis and the Conrad offer. They are three very different five-star resorts and each has its own charm and strengths. Choose the one that excites you most and factor in what you want to spend.

If you find the 5-star resorts too pricy, you'll be pleased to know that we highlight the best features of other Bora Bora resorts which also offer a vacation of a lifetime. Do keep in mind that, although Bora Bora became so famous for thatched-roof overwater bungalows we've had outstanding vacations in on-land accommodation too. If you have difficulty deciding, consider splitting your stay between two resorts or two styles of accommodation.

THE BEST OF THE BEST BORA BORA RESORTS

The following compilation lists the most outstanding attractions in Bora Bora and the resorts which offer them. Decide which Bora Bora resort is best for you according to *what you most value.*

Choose a resort in the best location:

For the Best Bora Bora Sunsets

Conrad Nui Bora Bora Resort

Book a sunset-facing bungalow with a view to the western horizon and enjoy spectacular sunsets from your deck, the overwater Upa Upa bar, and the formal restaurant.

For Best Bora Bora Resort Snorkeling

Conrad Nui

The Conrad Nui Bora Bora Resort has the best resort snorkeling, straight from its beach and over water bungalows. Read more about it in our "Best Snorkeling" chapter.

Sofitel Private Island

The Sofitel Private Island Motu has large coral gardens, teeming with fish, on one side of the small motu. Guests can row there in a kayak. This is the most frequented coral gardens on lagoon excursions and, by staying here, you can visit at any time you want.

For the Best View of Mt Otemanu

- Four Seasons Bora Bora
- Intercontinental Thalasso Bora Bora
- Bora Bora Le Meridien
- Pearl Beach Resort Bora Bora
- Sofitel Private Island Resort

Note: You can see Mt Otemanu from the Conrad Bora Bora Nui Resort from: the hill top, the spa and a few over water bungalows on the eastern side of the resort.

For the Best Beach

- Conrad Nui has the best resort beach for swimming, snorkeling, and other water activities. It's one of the longest in Bora Bora and (unlike at most of the resorts) is a *natural* white-sand beach. The lush, hillside backdrop is alive with colorful flowering plants which contrast with the ancient, lava rocks.
- The Intercontinental Thalasso beach has a long, well-groomed shore line for reclining on loungers under a thatched-umbrella to soak up the vision of Mt Otemanu across the turquoise water.
- The Four Seasons beach has the most dramatic Mt Otemanu view and a sandy islet that you can swim to from the beach.

For the Best Pool

Conrad Nui

The biggest pool in Bora Bora is also the newest! It has multiple levels with wide dress-circle views over the beach and out to the lagoon horizon. The pool area offers: a swim-up bar, glamourous cabanas, water-submerged sunbeds, and shady sunken lounges with access to a tasty cocktail and nibbles menu. This is the kind of pool you can spend all day (or all week) at.

Four Seasons

The Four Seasons pool trumps the Conrad's pool with its supreme view. This wave shaped pool is set among towering palms and has beach and mountain views. Elegant and private pool cabanas provide a space to relax out of the sun. You will have drag yourself out of the water to order a cocktail, which is the only downside to this magnificent area of the resort.

Pearl Beach

The lovely pool at Pearl Beach resort weaves around colourful tropical gardens and has amazing views across to Mt Otemanu. It doesn't have the facilities of some other pools in Bora Bora but its surrounds and aspect are beautiful enough for it to be listed in the top 3.

For the Best Spa Indulgence

- Intercontinental Resort incorporates a Thalasso Spa which utilizes deep ocean water in extraordinary pools and treatments.
- The Pearl Beach Resort treatment rooms are set on stilts over a tranquil lily pond and surrounded by tropical gardens.
- Four Seasons has a cathedral-like spa setting and offers the most indulgent treatment room for couples. The beautiful relaxation areas dedicated to men and women have sensational ocean and Mt Otemanu views.
- Conrad's hill-top spa has million-dollar views across the lagoon to the horizon, providing on-top-of-the-world panoramic pampering.
- The St Regis Resort has the spa in seclusion on its own private motu surrounded by the inner lagoon for snorkeling. The spa beach, with distant Mt Otemanu views is the loveliest part of this property.

CHOOSING A "ROOM"

*In Bora Bora you don't just get a room! Your villa
or bungalow will have separate areas for relaxing,
sleeping, dining and bathing. Your "room" can be
surrounded by lagoon, on the beach, or amongst
lush tropical gardens.*

After you have selected your perfect resort, it's time to choose between "room" options. There's no such thing as booking a "room" at Bora Bora resorts. They offer bungalows and villas, and some have a pool. Only two places on the island have some hotel-block style of accommodation, and even those have thatched roofs. Most people dream of staying in an idyllic overwater hut on the blue lagoon. But we'll share other wonderful "room" choices that provide the novelty of sleeping under a romantic, thatched-roof too. The four main 'room' styles in Bora Bora are:

- Over water bungalow
- Beach bungalow
- Garden bungalow
- Luxury villa with 2 or 3 bedrooms

BEST OVERWATER BUNGALOWS

Undoubtedly, Bora Bora has been made so famous by photographs of little thatched huts hovering over bright turquoise. But some of these overwater huts are not *little* – or even *huts*. They are luxurious overwater villas with multiple rooms and it's a jaw-dropping surprise to step inside! Some have a traditional, Polynesian feel while others provide a classical, European décor or a chic, modern interior. An overwater bungalow vacation will be very different to any hotel holiday that you've had in your life. There are things you may not even know that you need to know about choosing a "room" over water.

Biggest Bungalows and Villas

The standard villas at St Regis are the largest overwater bungalows in all of Tahiti. The bedrooms and bathrooms ooze an opulence of times gone by, when only the rich could afford to reside in such comfort. If you want more space than these overwater villas provide, you will need to pick between a Presidential overwater villa at the Conrad or one of the new luxurious Brando's at the Intercontinental Thalasso. You can also choose to stay in spacious villa *on land* at either St Regis or Four Seasons.

Newest over water bungalows

- Conrad Nui
- Intercontinental Thalasso Resort & Spa
- Four Seasons

Choose any of the immaculate Conrad Nui bungalows or one of the recently constructed, Intercontinental "Brando" bungalows for an over water bungalow that has been completely refurbished or newly built, in 2017.

The Four Seasons resort, constructed in 2008, was the newest resort to be built in Bora Bora. Their stylish villas were superbly designed and there's an on-going project for replacing thatched roofs which have a limited life in this hot, humid climate.

Bungalow Décor & Facilities

Looking for an authentic Polynesian "feel"? Or do you want a more 5-star international type of luxury? All the Bora Bora resorts use Polynesian features, artistry, and natural building materials but they also weave their own style into the décor. Standard overwater bungalow facilities include access to the water, a deck with sun-lounges, and separate bathroom and bedroom. Extra facilities can include: separate living room, outdoor dining areas, glass floors and private pontoons.

Conrad Nui

The Conrad is chic and stylish, with the most modern bungalow décor in Bora Bora. The facilities speak more of 5-star luxury than Polynesian style yet the use of natural materials and the extensive, tropical gardens around the resort give a distinct feeling of being in island paradise. The bungalow interiors feel very slick, yet also have an earthiness from the contrast of light and dark wood. The decks have been designed with large areas for relaxing and enjoying the lagoon, including a catamaran net for lying over the water. The deck is the highlight of a bungalow, and as travelers go to Bora Bora to see the lagoon, this is very appropriate. We were most impressed with the new Conrad Bungalows. They're perfectly designed for couples to have a sublime time for a whole week.

Four Seasons

The classy Four Seasons bungalows feature light timber throughout their lovely interiors. Their villas have an exceptional layout and are loaded with luxurious, romantic touches. They have windows to the lagoon below in the bathroom and a sitting nook in the bedroom. Generous outdoor living space is conveniently arranged on the decks and they have ample areas for both sunning and sitting in soothing shade. The large private pontoon is perfect for enjoying the lagoon and climbing in and out. These bungalows are also spaced further apart than at other resorts, so give more peace and privacy.

St Regis

The St Regis Resort opened with the promise of bringing opulence to Bora Bora. The bungalows were designed with the distinction of being impressively large, and lauded as the largest in Tahiti. They were two and three times the size of the other overwater bungalows available at that time. Their décor incorporates lots of rich, dark wood and a has a double layer of full curtains at the windows.

The most romantic inclusion is the vast four-poster bed which has a fabric canopy overhead. There are small windows to the lagoon in the floor of the bungalow, including one under the coffee-table in the living room. The large deck has a pair of sun-lounges in the prime position just a few steps outside the bedroom and living room doors. The dining table, with a thatched-roof for cover, has been situated further out. We noticed that while sitting there we felt more exposed to neighbors, passing water-traffic and the weather than at other resorts. Alongside the table area there are steps down to a private pontoon below.

Le Meridien

The bungalow size at Le Meridien is a modest 570 square feet. These Polynesian huts don't have a separate living room, just a sitting nook facing the bed. Their claim to fame is that they offer the largest, glass floor-panels of any bungalows in Tahiti. While sitting on the couch, guests can easily view any marine life passing below. We think that these villas give good value as their decor is chic, bright, airy, and modern. Plus, most of your time in Bora Bora will likely be enjoyed in the grand outdoors, around, in or on, the awesome lagoon!

Le Meridien is the place to stay if having a big window to the water-world underneath is most important to you. I should also shout out that you'll also have some of the best views of Mt Otemanu to be found around the island; from the restaurants, pool, and beach. Because Le Meridien is a sister resort to St Regis, you can also enjoy a free courtesy shuttle to dine at Lagoon up at St Regis. If you don't wish to sleep five-star, check out what else we say about this lovely resort. There's no need to max out your credit card to be surrounded by jaw-dropping, 5-star views of Bora Bora and Mt Otemanu!

Intercontinental Thalasso

A distinguishing feature of the Thalasso resort is that all accommodation is in overwater bungalows and the original ones are all the same, they just have different outlooks on the pontoons. It's a very egalitarian resort. These lovely bungalows are in clear, turquoise water with a soft, sandy floor. Providing 1000 square feet of classy vacation space, they're considerably bigger and more classically dressed than those at Le Meridien. They have exceptionally large windows in the separate living room, the bedroom and in front of the bath. A veil of curtain gives privacy when you wish to see out, without others seeing in. This makes the most of their outlook and sets the scene for romance. The well-designed decks have large covered areas for relaxing outdoor in comforts. Arty dried branches, used as railings, compliment the seascape and make these bungalows very photogenic.

Intercontinental Le Moana

If you are coming to Bora Bora on a budget and want to feel immersed in the true Polynesia, but with the comforts of a hotel stay, then this resort is a good option.

The traditional Polynesian construction of the bungalows gives them a quaint, artistic, air that's quite romantic. On stepping inside, there's a couch (which can become a bed) and a writing desk. A traditional, woven panel pulls across to separate the bedroom. These bungalows also have a coffee table that lifts open to feed the fish below.

One category of bungalows has a horizon view (all the way to my favourite little isle, Taha'a) and these offer the most privacy. Don't expect luxury though, come here for a more simple, earthy, Polynesian vacation with the little extras that a resort includes. It's not an ideal honeymoon location. "Humble with authentic Polynesian craftmanship" is how we describe Le Moana's arty, immaculate bungalows.

Le Moana gave us our very first resort-stay, back when we were feeling the call of Bora Bora and had less dollars to spend on a holiday. Last vacation we stayed there for 2 nights to have easy access while checking out places on the main island. We had to seriously adjust our expectations after staying at 5-star resorts but we were high on life and nostalgia and it still had a certain something.

Pearl Beach Resort

Pearl Beach is another distinctively Polynesian resort. The overwater bungalows are quite small but provide just enough room for two – providing you don't want to tango. A traditional Polynesian artistry, that's both functional and aesthetically beautiful, is evident in every detail of these unique bungalows. Inside they are bright and airy with a light-wood-and-white theme. Tapas hangings decorate the walls and continue to share popular Polynesian legends. Their deck area is a cosy size and has 2 sun beds, a small built-in table and a mini personal pontoon.

From the bungalows, the view across to Bora Bora Island is absolutely awesome and shows a different perspective to any other resort. You see the mountain and a silhouette of the Walk of Kings. These bungalows provide cheap, resort-style accommodation in Bora Bora and, considering Bora Bora prices, are worth the money you pay. But don't expect luxury. Staying in one of these is all about the Polynesian feel, a fantastic beach, lagoon access, and views you will remember for a lifetime!

Sofitel Private Island

The Private Island overwater bungalows are indeed private and peaceful, as this is a tiny resort on a very small isle. They're set along one pontoon which begins at the shallow beach and follows the motu's coastline. Some bungalows have a surprising up-close–and-personal view of rocky Mt Otemanu looking down over the resort from high above. The bungalows have been refurbished, retaining a timeless, Polynesian feel. Although they are much smaller than the villas at 5-star resorts, there's still a feeling of exclusivity around this unique resort. The one main room with a sitting nook is all that a couple in love, vacationing in Bora Bora, actually needs. You can enjoy the romance and intimacy of sleeping over the world's most beautiful lagoon in a thatched roof hut, awake to sensational views, and climb down your ladder for a refreshing start to the day. The little deck provides 2 sunbeds, ample cover, and a small area for entering the lagoon.

Rooms with the Best View

The easiest way to ensure you are booking a room with a spectacular view of Bora Bora's treasured peak, is to make sure that your room includes the words "Otemanu" or "Mountain view". These are the rooms in the best view category at the resorts:

- Four Seasons Otemanu Bungalow Over Water Suite (with pool) and Mountain View Overwater Suite
- St Regis Deluxe Overwater Otemanu View
- Sofitel Private Island Luxury Bungalow Horizon Overwater
- Le Meridien Premium Otemanu View Bungalow
- Intercontinental Thalasso Diamond Otemanu View Overwater Villa or Brando Suite.
- Pearl Beach Otemanu View Overwater Suite & Otemanu View Beach Suite

ESSENTIAL TIPS FOR THE BEST OVERWATER BUNGALOW STAY

1. Don't make the mistake of thinking that it's cheaper to book a budget-priced

overwater bungalow on the main island of Tahiti, or Moorea; the experience will not be the same. Choose a bungalow over the Bora Bora Lagoon to be above the most calm, blue water in the world. If your budget can't stretch to an overwater bungalow in Bora Bora, you'll likely get more pleasure from a similar priced beach bungalow at a Bora Bora resort like Le Meridien, Le Moana or Pearl Beach.

2. If you want to jump for joy – straight off your deck into turquoise water – book a bungalow further from shore, at a resort where the lagoon is deep enough.

3. Beach babies may want to have a villa close to the resort's beach. These are in shallower water so it's easier to swim to the beach from them.

4. Be aware that only one luxury resort, the Conrad, has abundant living coral around the overwater bungalows. If it's important to see colorful tropical fish swimming below your bungalow, or have superb snorkeling straight from your deck, the Nui is for you. Otherwise you may only see a very occasional stingray passing underneath.

5. If you *don't* want to climb down the ladder from your deck into water with interesting creatures you may prefer a resort without coral. The resorts on the eastern ring of motus have very little coral. The overwater villas at the Intercontinental Thalasso are above an area of lagoon that's like a turquoise swimming pool with a clear, sandy bottom. Several resorts on the east side have lagoonariums with marine biologists to introduce guests to the sea life and assist them with feeling comfortable with sharing the lagoon.

6. Those seeking quiet seclusion can choose a villa facing the lagoon rather than one facing the resort. Some resorts offer "Horizon" overwater villas. Examples from quite different price brackets are 5-star Conrad Nui and Polynesian Le Moana. They are also in separate areas of the lagoon yet each has a category that looks right across the lagoon to the reef and ocean beyond, all the way to the horizon. If you are keen to have maximum privacy, simply upgrade to a bungalow at the end of the pier.

7. Want the thrill of relaxing on your romantic, bungalow deck while the sun sets over the watery horizon? French Polynesians refer to the "sunset side" of an island and that's where you need to stay. Conrad Nui is the only resort in Bora Bora where guests can have that sublime, almost-spiritual experience.

8. Do you fancy lazing on a blow-up watermelon or pineapple floatie, tied to your bungalow? You need to take the current movements under your overwater villa into account. The further from shore your over water bungalow is, the more chance the current will be stronger. In winter, there's a current flowing, from the west side of the lagoon, past the St Regis and Four Seasons resorts. Request a bungalow on the western side of the pontoon or you'll be floating under the pontoon.

9. Are you stretching your finances to have your dream of an overwater bungalow stay, and an on-land villa simply won't do? Food and drinks can be pricey too, so you can save on that by staying at a resort with easy access to the main island, where more food options are available and you can eat where the locals eat. Another way that you can usually save some money on meals is by including breakfast or half board when you book. Keep in mind that the breakfast buffet at

resorts is a feast to graze upon, and if you indulge in the morning, you'll likely be so satisfied that you may share a dish at lunch or even forget to eat.

11. An over water bungalow stay invites relaxation. Don't cut the benefits short. Stay at least 5 nights so that you can unpack and unwind. For the evenings bring some movies you have been wanting to see. Borrowing from reception is free. Watch a movie in bed with the water lapping gently lapping your cares away, underneath.

11. Here's a hint for those planning a honeymoon on a budget. Don't book a "cheap" overwater bungalow such as those offered at Le Maitai or Sofitel Marara. You'll get more pleasure from a similar priced beach bungalow at a better Bora Bora resort.

12. In Paradise *even* some of the bungalows *over* water have their own private pool. There's something incredibly decadent about relaxing in a pool surrounded by lagoon – but is it worth the cost? The lagoon around your bungalow is like a big, turquoise swimming pool so if you love being in sea water you will prefer the lagoon to a small swimming pool. However, those who want a contained space to cool off or relax without sea-creatures, a current, or salt water, will be ecstatic to have the convenience of a pool on their deck. We mostly use the pool in the evening after dark. It's a beautiful place to relax in the arms of your lover and watch the sunset.

13. One of the most romantic experiences to be found in Tahiti can only be enjoyed with an overwater bungalow stay. At many resorts you can book a breakfast to be delivered by a flower-decorated canoe, sometimes to the strumming of a ukulele. Keep this a secret and surprise your honey.

Beach or Garden bungalow

Beach and garden villas are a smart choice for budget-conscious travelers who desire a resort vacation without paying top dollar. Guests staying in a beach or garden villa get a wonderful deal. They have access to the same beautiful beach, lagoon, pool, views, and luxurious resort facilities as overwater bungalow guests but likely pay half the price to be there. The on-land bungalows always have more space, inside and around them, than the over water bungalows. At some resorts you can step straight out of your door onto pure, white sand.

Beach and garden bungalows are the best option for those vacationing with young children. As well has providing more space for a family, they are a safer option as overwater bungalows have decks without railings. Most Bora Bora resorts do not allow young children to stay in overwater bungalows, and if they do, they usually request that parents sign a waiver.

On-land options can give more freedom to go on some of the island's unique excursions too. It feels easier to leave the resort and more affordable to take excursions, when you're paying less to be there.

The beach bungalows at Le Meridien and Pearl Beach are both in superb locations for catching astounding views of Mt Otemanu (from opposite sides of the island). Each resort has a completely different bungalow interior. Le Meridien's bungalows have been smartly restored with a light, airy, modern interior. Pearl Beach takes pride in giving visitors an authentic Polynesian décor and utilizing many natural materials to dress up their garden-isle bungalows.

Luxury villa (2-3 bedrooms)

Those coming as a group or family have awesome choices too. Most Bora Bora resorts have luxurious villa options with 2 or 3 bedrooms. Villas with extra bedrooms usually provide more bathrooms, living space and privacy, plus they often come with a plunge pool, and some even have their own private beach (if they are located on land). Some resorts have fantastic on-land accommodation which, when you consider what it offers, may give you a superior vacation for less money than what overwater accommodation would cost.

WHY ARE YOU STAYING IN BORA BORA?

Before leaving this topic, we want to remind you that deciding which resort to stay at is simply the most critical choice to be made for determining the quality of your vacation. One of the biggest joys of visiting a dream island, like Bora Bora, is the adventure of staying in accommodation entirely different to what you have, back home. Visitors can experience that at every resort in Bora Bora. But here are some important considerations:

- Are you mostly coming to frolic around the infamous lagoon and don't need to stay 5-star to have an extraordinary time? You'll be pleased to know that there are significant savings to be made by staying at a 4-star resort in Bora Bora. We suggest you compare the lovely 4-star resorts and decide which one appeals to you.
- Are you coming for a honeymoon or a really special occasion? Have you only ever stayed 5-star and have fixed, high standards? Then don't decide to stay down-star just because Bora Bora appears to cost more than some other destinations. Bora Bora is an extraordinary island with unique accommodation and adventures. You'll discover that many of the pleasures

you indulge in are actually priceless! Many of the most superb experiences and memories will be created and enjoyed around your resort. We strongly suggest choosing the resort with the most stars you can pay for.

- Staying at a classier resort may mean that you opt out from having a pool on the deck or choose to check into the delights of a villa on land. Overall the on-land villas are much better value. If you want more ideas for how to make your dream vacation possible, we specifically reveal a wealth of tips to keep more money in your purse *and* have an exciting Bora Bora vacation in our book "What Your travel Agent May Not Tell You About Bora Bora". Why should beautiful Bora Bora only be a playground to the rich and famous!

- To add to the beat of this "how to choose" drum we'd like to share that Pacific for Less, the specialist Tahiti travel agency, which we trust and highly recommend (for getting the best prices and inclusions when booking) insists that their clients (who are virtually all honeymooners) book 4-star or 5-star resorts. Their team knows that they can rely on "oohs" and "aahs" of certain satisfaction from those who stay at this level. The agency principal is passionately "hands on" and says that your honeymoon is too important to take a gamble. The only 4-star resorts that she can confidently book are the Sofitel Private Island and Le Meridien.

THE BEST SNORKELING
IN BORA BORA

*Bora Bora has beautiful coral gardens around the
lagoon. But don't assume that you'll be able to
swim off your resort's beach and immerse yourself
in a coral garden.*

Bora Bora has many beautiful coral gardens but getting to most of them requires a trip in a boat as, to capture the most sensational views, the resorts have based themselves around the sandy motus that fringe the lagoon. This means that most of them are not located in areas with coral gardens. This is a good thing for the environment as they minimize the impact on the health of the reefs by maintaining some distance. Two resorts have been built in areas that host thriving coral, and these resorts have put extra care into conservation and encouraging new coral growth.

If you want to enjoy the best snorkeling in the lagoon you have two options – stay at a one of the resorts with good snorkeling nearby or book a snorkeling excursion and be whisked away by a guide to the best snorkeling spots in the lagoon. Even if you do stay at a resort with good snorkeling, we advise you to take a snorkeling excursion that shows you around the amazing lagoon.

To bring coral to their resorts, many Bora Bora resorts have created their own lagoon environment with an eco-system very similar to that in the lagoon. They call these lagoonariums, and they are the next best thing to snorkeling in the coral gardens in the lagoon. You will find many species of fish, coral and coral nurseries within the lagoonariums, but you will not find any sharks or sting rays. This is good news for those who are a little nervous about unfamiliar sea-creatures!

Lagoonariums are fantastic places for beginner snorkelers and children to enjoy explorative, playful time in the water. If you choose a resort with a large lagoonarium, you could happily spend some time in it each day and see something different. But if you are brave enough and comfortable with your gear, make sure you venture out of the resort lagoonarium and into the real lagoon at some time during your trip. Nothing compares to the beauty of being out in the Bora Bora lagoon.

RESORTS WITH THE BEST SNORKELING

Although all the resorts are on picture-postcard beaches around the lagoon, only one resort in Bora Bora has living coral along its natural white-sand beach. Another resort has Bora Bora's most popular coral gardens, just a short row around the tiny motu. Because snorkeling is such a popular activity, some resorts have created inner lagoonariums with coral nurseries, for guests to snorkel in. Others have implemented coral regeneration programs to encourage coral to grow near their over water bungalows. Some resorts employ a marine biologist, dedicated to the program.

From the Beach & Bungalows

Conrad Bora Bora Nui

Keen to snorkel straight from the beach or your overwater bungalow? Conrad Nui is the only resort with abundant coral heads under the overwater bungalows and all along the beach. It's Gloria's pick for the best resort snorkeling. Overwater guests can have the delight of snorkeling straight from their bungalow deck and all Nui guests enjoy easy access to prime snorkeling just by walking a few meters into the lagoon from the beach. Anyone who can swim will have a marvelous snorkeling journey by floating from the overwater bungalows, at one end of the beach, all the way down to the black lava rocks at the other end of the resort. It's a very exciting "ride". Small children can have fun sitting at the water's edge and making friends with the tiny fish dart inquisitively around their feet.

Sofitel Private Island

The Sofitel Private Island has, what tour guides rate, the best coral gardens in the Bora Bora lagoon, just off the shoreline. Guests can paddle a kayak from the resort's beach around to the south side of the motu and swim to the most visited coral gardens in Bora Bora which is nicknamed "the Aquarium". Much of the day you can have it all to yourself. This is Melinda's pick for the best resort snorkeling. You can do it leisurely, as often as you want, without cost, and it's always teeming with fish. The short, scenic row is also incredible fun if you're up for a little adventure. With Mount Otemanu touring above, we found this an ultimate, water-fun experience.

Intercontinental Le Moana

Intercontinental Le Moana is in a shallow part of the lagoon at the southern tip of the main island. For years this resort has been fostering a coral regeneration program near the overwater bungalows (which each have a glass floor panel to view the lagoon. Guests can also stroll across the road to Matira Beach for some good snorkeling.

Four Seasons Resort

The Four Seasons Resort has a few coral heads at the very end of the western overwater bungalows. But most beginner snorkelers will have a more interesting time in the resort's inner lagoon which can also be explored with a marine biologist.

Pearl Beach Resort

Pearl Beach Resort has also had a marine biologist working at regenerating coral near the overwater bungalows. The coral is still quite small but has attracted some colorful fish.

The Intercontinental Thalasso Resort

The Intercontinental Thalasso Resort has a scattering of coral heads in front of the chapel. As they provide a home for a variety of fish, the area is fun for those building their confidence. Keen snorkelers will want to see more by taking a lagoon excursion with snorkeling stops.

The Best Resort Lagoonariums

There is almost no coral growing naturally on the east side of the lagoon; the water is a brilliant blue and has a sandy bottom. Most of the resorts in this area have created artificial lagoons and employ a marine biologist for the prime purpose of nurturing coral to establish colonies of tropical fish for guests to explore.

Le Meridien

Le Meridian has a very large inner lagoon with abundant coral and fish. The sheltered water also serves as a turtle sanctuary and you can book a session for swimming amongst the turtles with the marine biologist. This is a perfect place for beginner snorkelers and anyone who's not comfortable exploring underwater in the main lagoon.

St Regis Resort

St Regis offers the best lagoonarium snorkeling experience. A large inner lagoon winds around the small isle where the spa is situated. You can float along with the current for a drift snorkel adventure and discover beautiful coral and colorful fish. The big star of the St Regis Lagoon is Maeve, a massive, blue/purple Napoleon fish who has become quite a pet. It's an amazing experience to play "Where is Maeve?" and snorkel along next to her. Each day a marine biologist gives a scheduled talk which is worth attending to learn more about Maeva and the eco system in the lagoon. As the biologist has built a very close relationship with Maeva she rushes into the shallow water "on call", like a puppy dog, and reveals an astonishing neon turquoise that would camouflage her in the brilliant blues of the main lagoon.

Four Seasons Resort

The Four Seasons resort also maintains a fascinating lagoonarium. The coral nursery is presented on submerged sculptures, like a living art installation. A resident marine biologist gives snorkeling tours of the Sanctuary Lagoon each day and there's a tour especially for children. The biologist shows coral grafting, gives fish-feeding sessions and discusses the island's ecosystem, to educate visitors about the unique lagoon environment that makes Bora Bora so famous. Guests may also explore on their own. The Four Seasons lagoonarium is the easiest to enter and exit as it has a gently sloping sandy beach to wade easily in.

Our favorite Bora Bora Resort
Snorkeling

After snorkeling at all the resorts, we find it difficult to choose one favorite, as each gives a totally different experience. The Conrad Nui offers the best natural coral gardens right along its beach. But we also consider the Sofitel Private Island a top pick for snorkeling, providing you're active and adventurous. The coral gardens at the back of the motu are stunning and the scenery as we paddled around was "Pinch me, is this real?" beautiful! The whole experience is so memorable that it's worth putting in a little effort.

The resort with the best snorkeling in a lagoonarium is the St Regis. The body of water is so long and large that it feels like being in a real lagoon. Searching for, and swimming with Maeva was most entertaining. She has become so tame that if she was released into the main lagoon a fisherman would quickly catch her.

Four Seasons lagoon is a close second as their Sanctuary Lagoon seems straight out of Disneyworld. There are shaded sun-lounges on a perfect beach to leave your things on; and a gentle, sandy slope to enter the water and discover coral and fish.

BEST LAGOON SNORKELING

Here are the best places to snorkel in the Bora Bora lagoon. Some of them will require you to take a lagoon snorkelling excursion to get there.

The "Aquarium"

It's not surprising that the Bora Bora's most frequented coral gardens happens to have the best lagoon snorkeling to be found. It's in an area of the lagoon that's more protected in the event of a very bad storm. This explains why there's an abundance of living coral to give homes to a multitude of fish. The water is a stunning bright turquoise-blue. Underneath you can discover zebra fish, moray eels, stingrays, colourful coral and tropical fish of many colours. To snorkel at the "Aquarium" you must stay at the Sofitel Private Island, hire a boat, or book a snorkeling excursion. Almost every lagoon excursion we have been on has stopped off there so you're likely be treated to a visit, whichever excursion provider you choose.

Southern tip of Bora Bora

The coral at the very southern reef of Bora Bora is the most colourful around. Pink, purple, yellow and green coral abounds. There is less marine life in this area of the lagoon, due to the serious storm that passed nearby in the Pacific, in 2010, but the luminous coral makes up for that. Lonesome stingrays are also seen in this area and an occasional, small, reef shark. The coral has been frequently damaged by strong currents so, depending upon the current health of the coral, the excursion providers decide whether to take guests to this place. It's possible to swim to this area directly from Matira Beach, if you are a very competent snorkeler.

Hotel Bora Bora

As it was the first hotel to be built on the island, the site chosen for Hotel Bora Bora was above a thriving coral garden. Many folks around the world have nostalgic memories of their first Bora Bora visits when they stayed at this original hotel. They tell of enjoying amazing snorkeling, directly under the overwater bungalows. Even though the resort is closed, it's still possible to snorkel around this area from Matira Beach. Although it's not an area that snorkeling excursions visit, you can explore on your own.

Manta Ray Trench

It's an extraordinary experience to float above the well-known manta ray trench and peer down and see the walls of the lagoon drop off on each side of you, and then plunge into darkness, because of the depth. To stop at this place, you will need to book a lagoon excursion with a snorkelling focus. The water is very deep and most excursions do not take guests there. If you want to see this location, check with your provider before you book. On a lucky day – as you gaze down into the dull depths – you will see the dark silhouette of manta rays circling or gliding in what locals playfully call a "ray ballet". It's possible to see manta rays in other deeper areas of the lagoon too. But if you can get to this area in the early morning, there is a much better chance of spotting them here.

Outside the Pass

This isn't snorkeling in the lagoon – but it's such an incredible experience that we recommend it as a snorkeling stop not to be missed! The weather needs to be calm for the excursion provider to take the small boat outside the pass and into the Pacific Ocean. A short way out, on the other side of the reef, there's an area frequented by snorkelers and scuba divers. Here you can float in royal-blue, crystal-clear water amongst dozens of graceful reef sharks. The real stars out here are the large lemon sharks that will usually make an appearance.

BEST DINING AND BARS

Most visitors to Bora Bora aren't aware of the diverse dining options that are available. You can eat like a local, taste exotic cuisine, savour French delicacies, feast on Polynesian fare, and dine like royalty.

There's an elegant simplicity to the nightlife in Bora Bora. For most of the year evenings are balmy and the stars shine more brightly than any other place I've been. It's a time to hold hands and watch the golden orb sink slowly into the glistening ocean, before indulging in some exotic food. Listening to the enlivening music at resort bars, while sipping Tahiti cocktails with your beloved, is intoxicating. This is one of the most romantic beach getaways on earth!

Getting around at the end of the day is pleasurable. It's cooler, and the fragrant perfumes of tropical flowers waft on the gentle breeze. You can linger on the beach and stroll leisurely to your "pick" of the resort restaurants.

On the main island of Bora Bora there's also a variety of unique restaurants that are entertaining to visit. Most of them provide a complimentary pickup from your hotel or the shuttle-dock of your motu resort. They drop you back after eating, ensuring that you catch the last boat to your resort.

BEST RESTAURANTS

Best Main-Island Restaurants

Fare Manui (Lucky House)

This casual eatery offers friendly service and a varied menu of tasty food; including beef, pizza, seafood, shellfish, pasta and veggie dishes; at prices much cheaper than resort restaurants. It's *the* place in Bora Bora for delicious wood-fired pizza. Locals meet here and there's a full bar at the back by a swimming pool which was moved from the closed Bora Bora Hotel. Refreshments such as coconut water and Tahiti cocktails are cheaper than at resorts. Fare Manui is conveniently located, right by Matira Beach. Do catch the sunset before eating there. Food is reliably good, and you don't pay for views.

Restaurant St James

Restaurant St James, in the north of Vaitape on the mainland, provides intimate, twilight dinners overlooking the lagoon. You can book a pre-dinner sunset cruise in an outrigger canoe to watch the sun set, then be dropped off at Restaurant St James to enjoy a 3-course meal which is included in the cost. Combining these two experiences into one excursion gives a very romantic evening and makes it easy to get to this highly rated restaurant from your resort.

Matira Beach Restaurant

This casual, lagoon-side restaurant specializes in seafood that's presented with French flare. There's a wide choice of delectable dishes including: fillet and scallops, rib-eye with shrimp, crusted tuna, and spicy sushi. Awesome views of the 2 miles of beach (just outside the door) make eating here, either for lunch or while watching the sunset, a relaxing experience. It's run by a husband and wife team who strive to do everything with care. Don't be surprised if your friendly chef (owner) is also the driver of the courtesy shuttle back to your hotel. There are only a small number of tables, so make a booking in peak season.

Villa Mahana

Nestled on the mountainside of Bora Bora's main island, this unique restaurant artfully blends French tradition with a tropical island freshness, in both its food and fanciful atmosphere. Under chef Damien, Villa Mahana has earned and maintained a much-lauded reputation for fine French cuisine, laced with island ingredients. The fame is deserved, and this restaurant is the most popular one for those wanting to splurge on a memorable meal outside their resort. Diners can choose from the exotic 5 course menu with wine pairings or eat a la carte. Whether you order melt-in-the mouth mahi mahi or beef tenderloin, the sauces are divine. Only a few tables are set up each evening so, to ensure a place, we suggest that you make reservations a few months in advance.

Best Resort Restaurants

Four Seasons Fare Hoa Beach Bar & Grill

Fare Hoa offers open-air eating under a thatched roof, surrounded by palms. It's an ocean away from the usual air-conditioning, kitchen clatter, and noisy acoustics of restaurants back home.

During the day this restaurant exudes a beach-club feeling and, in the evening, it transforms to a lounge atmosphere with live music arousing a blissful, vacation mood.

All the food we ate here during our stay was delicious and the exceptional, entertaining service made each meal an occasion. We think that it's well priced for Bora Bora. Four Seasons has opened this restaurant up to guests from outside the resort (except during peak season). This means that folk from other hotels can now book to dine at Fare Hoa for a fun meal amongst the magical beauty of the Four Seasons grounds. There will be a charge for the shuttle service but it's worth the cost to see this amazing resort.

St Regis Bam Boo

The current chef at St Regis is Chinese so it was no surprise that some of the tastiest food on offer can be found in the Asian restaurant. Sushi is made with freshly caught fish, and the creative presentation of all dishes makes them colourful works of art. The menu has recently been updated and now includes traditional Chinese wok dishes and teppanyaki options.

St Regis Lagoon Restaurant

The spectacular location and décor, creative cuisine, and excellent service, make Lagoon one of the most talked about restaurants in Bora Bora.

A feature of this glamorous restaurant is the glass floor panel with lights illuminating the turquoise lagoon. Diners can view reef sharks, attracted by the light, swimming by. They're for entertainment only, not on the menu!

On balmy evenings the ambiance while dining on the deck is sublime. Book for the earliest time possible and add more romance to the evening by showing up in the gleaming bar around 5.30pm to sip pre-dinner drinks while watching the sun set over Bora Bora Island. Visitors staying at other resorts are welcome to dine here too. There is a charge for the shuttle service.

Conrad Nui Tamure Beach Grill

The casual Tamure Beach Grill has been one of our favourite Bora Bora restaurants for many years. It served as an all-day restaurant when Nui was a Hilton but now it's open for lunch. We were pleased to find that they have continued to serve the best dishes that were previously on the menu as well as adding some tasty options. There are so many choices that it would be easy to eat here every lunch of your vacation and not taste everything. We're still dreaming of curried prawns with lemon rice and the fresh tuna dishes that we were served. If you're staying at the splendid new Nui, you'll be blessed with delectable choices for a feet-in-the-sand (or water) lunch each day.

Most Romantic Dinner locations

- Villa Mahana – ask for the (one and only) outside table up the top
- Restaurant St James – ask for a table alongside the water
- Lagoon by Jean George at St Regis – reserve a table outside for 6pm sharp
- Room service – on your overwater bungalow balcony
- Romantic private dinner for two on the beach – book this through your resort before your vacation

Best Resort Bars

Conrad Nui Pool Bar

The Conrad Bora Bora Nui has recently opened with two sensational new bars which are now our favorite in Bora Bora. The day-time Pool Bar has swim up stools and sunken seating nooks (where you can also order the lunch menu) alongside the pool. While relaxing in this heavenly setting you can see all the way across the lagoon and ocean to the horizon.

Conrad Nui Upa Upa Bar

The other outstanding bar at the Conrad Bora Bora Nui is the overwater Upa Upa Lounge situated out over the lagoon. Upa Upa has the island's most panoramic seats to the sun setting over the ocean. This is simply *the* best place to be at sunset in Bora Bora – unless you're one of the lucky few who are staying in a Conrad Presidential overwater villa! Tasting cocktails at the Upa Upa Bar is lots of fun. Each of the bar staff have personally designed one. You can order from the menu or select a liquor or flavor and the talented bartender will work his magic to create a cocktail unlike any you've tasted before. The snack menu is fresh and tasty, with plenty of variety to graze for a meal.

Four Seasons Sunset Bar

The Sunset Bar at the Four Seasons serves unique cocktail creations and freshly made sushi in a spectacular location. Those escaping from the city can have a dream date-night night at the Sunset Bar. Set lagoon-side, its charming decor combines *sophistication* with *island*. There's a choice of perching up at an interactive bar, lounging indoors in cushioned comfort, or romancing your partner out on the over water terrace – while nibbling on very fresh sushi and tapas, as the sun silhouettes the main island.

If your over water bungalow doesn't face the sunset, it's a great place to be around 5pm. In winter you can witness the golden globe sinking into the water, on the right side of the main island. It's the prime location around the resort to relax and enjoy a drink before going to another restaurant for dinner. Or you can stay on and have sushi if you want a light evening meal.

Best Bars on the Main Island

Bora Bora Yacht Club

You don't have to sail in through the pass and moor a yacht to be welcome at the Bora Bora Yacht Club. It's a place where locals and visitors can chat together with seafarers traversing the Pacific Ocean. We've met some out-of-the-ordinary characters there! Visitors can have a complimentary pick-up from hotels on the main island and the shuttle bases of motu resorts. Just ask someone at the front desk to ring for it.

This casual, open-air venue makes the most of the lagoon-side environment to serve up a well-priced lunch or dinner, and the cocktails are cheaper than at resorts. The wide views west, all the way to the watery horizon, mean that this spot vies with Conrad's Upa Upa Bar for best place to observe the sun set over the Pacific Ocean. On very hot days you can sit at tables, partially submerged in water, to cool down. In the evening, part of the entertainment is watching manta rays and stingrays, that are attracted by the light, as they pass by.

EAT LIKE A LOCAL

Les Roulottes

To have a snippet of authentic life in French Polynesia, try eating where the locals eat. In Vaitape and Matira Beach small stands called "snacks" sell burgers, roast chicken, pizza, crepes and take-out Tahitian Chinese dishes.

Each evening mobile diners set up in Vaitape village serving grilled fish, steak and fries, kebabs, barbecued chicken legs, and poisson cru. They're called Les Roulottes which literally means "rolling food trucks". Roulottes provide tables and chairs for eating outdoors. They're a tradition throughout the islands of Tahiti. Visitors can enjoy tasty, cheap eating in Bora Bora by dining with the locals for around 1,200 XPF/$13 a meal.

Roadside Stands

As you're traveling around the main island, you will observe little stands on the roadside offering local fruits and freshly caught lagoon fish. Take the time to stop and treat yourself to some fresh island produce. This is the cheapest eating in Bora Bora. You'll have the freshest produce and help an enterprising Polynesian.

BORA BORA ESSENTIAL EXPERIENCES

*The isle of romance offers many pleasurable
activities and excursions that are uniquely Bora
Bora. Vacation time is precious so
book the ones you fancy, before you go.
Here are the top things to do on the world's most
beautiful island.*

TOP THINGS TO DO IN BORA BORA

Stay in an Over Water Bungalow

In 2017 French Polynesia celebrated 50 years of the iconic overwater bungalow. These thatched-roof huts over water were designed in French Polynesia and, as Bora Bora has the most perfect lagoon to situate them, it's little wonder that they became a symbol of Bora Bora. There are overwater bungalow options at every level of accommodation so don't miss out on this unique experience. If you're on a budget, stay in one for part of your vacation.

Snorkel the Coral Gardens

Bora Bora's best coral gardens are teeming with more fish than I've seen in any aquarium! Most coral gardens are out in Bora Bora's lagoon so visitors must book an excursion to see them. How many, and which stops you have on a snorkeling tour depends on the time of year, movement of sea life, health of the coral, and the tour provider you are with. Guests staying at Sofitel Private Island can row to the popular "Aquarium" coral gardens and, in their own time, enjoy this favorite spot for free.

Sail the Lagoon

This is something to reminisce about when you're back in the office! Getting out on the lagoon is the highlight of a Bora Bora vacation and the most tranquil way to enjoy it is by sailing boat. Vitamin Sea offers 2 sailing excursions; a morning or afternoon sailing with a floating bar experience; and the other is a very romantic sunset sail. Both these activities must be booked well ahead of going as opportunities are limited. We had such a memorable day, sailing Bora Bora's lagoon that Tom, my fiancé, declared this his favorite activity.

Picnic on a Motu

Motus are small coral islands in Bora Bora's lagoon. They are the quintessential vision of paradise – palm trees, white sand, and turquoise water – and offer dramatic views across the lagoon to the towering peak of Mt Otemanu. Having lunch on a motu gives an authentic taste of Polynesian life. Your host will prepare traditional Tahitian delicacies such as freshly caught, barbecued mahi mahi; tuna served Tahitian style with lime and coconut milk; marinated chicken; and juicy, tropical fruit. To experience lunch on a motu book a Bora Bora lagoon excursion that includes a motu picnic.

Swim with the Sharks

Yes, you read right! Swimming with the sharks *is* one of the top things to do in Bora Bora so don't miss out on this phenomenal experience! The Bora Bora lagoon is home to graceful, black-tipped reef sharks that are timid; but curious. Swimming with the sharks is a moment that you'll remember for the rest of your life, so be brave and book a shark and ray tour snorkeling tour.

Pat the Stingrays

Don't leave Bora Bora without making friends with the puppy dogs of the sea! All good lagoon excursions include a stop to feed the stingrays, and you will be amazed by how happy they are to meet you (or happy to be fed). You can meet and greet the sharks and stingrays on a lagoon snorkeling tour.

Take a 4WD Tour into the Inner Island

Bora Bora isn't just a beautiful lagoon. There's a vast inner island with intriguing history and legends that can only be explored through taking a 4WD tour. We'd been to Bora Bora many times before finally experiencing the adventure of a 4WD tour. The morning out was such fun and so interesting that we wondered why we hadn't taken this unique drive sooner.

Have a Professional Photoshoot

Where in the world can you find a background as striking as Bora Bora! But most visitors are couples and going as a couple means that one of you is always behind the camera. This is a very special occasion (which may only be lived once) so book a photo shoot with a professional photographer for a couple of hours. You'll treasure a record of creating memories together.

Dine Privately on the Beach

There's nothing more romantic than a dinner (or lunch) for two on the beach in Bora Bora. One vacation I had the lunch of my life on the Sofitel Private Island. It was so sensational that I dreamed of sharing this experience, with the love of my life. When I headed back to Bora Bora with my man, we booked a dinner for two on the secluded beach at St Regis spa. The evening was magical – so magical that Tommy proposed to me.

Get Married or Renew Your Vows

Although our proposal didn't turn into an elopement, it could have. The Bora Bora resorts have picturesque chapels for guests to marry in. There's also the option of getting married on a beach or motu. Ceremonies can be Polynesian or Western style, depending on your preference. Bora Bora weddings are often elopements or have just a small wedding party as witnesses. Ceremonies can either be symbolic or legal. But if you want your wedding in Bora Bora to be legal you will need to organize the paperwork months ahead of time.

Watch a Bora Bora Sunset

There's something momentous about the scene of the golden orb swelling and appearing to sink into ocean. I am mesmerized, despite how many times I've witnessed it! Most vacationers can't view this from hotels on the east side of the island and for years we were telling people to go to Matira beach at this time of day. But at the end of a recent vacation in Bora Bora I revisited Matira, to see the sunset view, and it was a big disappointment. The usually quiet, main area of the beach was crowded with folk who had the same idea. I mused that they must have all been reading BoraBoraIslandGuide.com because when we were there previously, we almost had the beach to ourselves at sunset! This time the actual view was quite narrow due to the sun's winter passage in the sky. It was setting at the far end of the beach and people were massed on the strip of sand, with cameras poised, taking photos of the silhouettes of other travelers taking photos of the golden sky.

A quieter place to view the sun setting over the sea is the Yacht Club. Located on the west side of the island, the open-air Yacht Club has panoramic views out across the pass to the ocean. We recently revisited this venue too. The panorama is still on display, the atmosphere is very "tropical island" and there's a bigger choice of chairs to relax in. You can just buy a drink if you wish. Previously we'd had delicious meals here. But on this occasion, we went as a group of five and not one of us was impressed with the quality of the food, although it looked good on the plates! On enquiring, we heard that the previous chef was on vacation. Fresh coconut pina coladas were no longer an option either.

A fun way to have front row seats to a sensational Bora Bora sunset is by booking a sunset cruise which takes you out on the lagoon. If you want more intimacy you can do this as a private tour. But you don't need to spend that big to have a big experience because we've found that a small group tour gives a memorable time too. The lighting in the sky creates an expectant mood and a hush comes over the boat as the sun swells and suddenly disappears. Some of these tours include a lagoon-side dinner which is a great way to smoothly combine a cruise and eating out.

Of course, if you stay at the Conrad Nui, you don't have to leave your resort – or even your luxurious bungalow – to have the grandest seats to glorious sunsets that can be found anywhere in Bora Bora.

Snorkel Outside the Reef

When you're on a lagoon tour, ask your guide to take the boat outside the reef for a plunge into the crystal clear, royal-blue ocean. You won't find such an awesome shade of blue in a box of Crayolas! I took my first "ray and shark watching" tour while my (then) boyfriend went on a diving excursion. The friendly Polynesian guide gave me the confidence to get in the water with the sharks and the experience was one of the most significant in my lifetime. The water was so transparent that it seemed as if I could see forever. I watched graceful sharks gliding about in their deep water-world and a pair of divers walking along the sandy ocean floor, way off in the distance. I'm such a "scaredy- cat" that I won't go on a roller coaster but now, when I see people remain in the boat, I feel sad about the pleasure they're missing. Small boats can only go outside the reef when the weather permits. If it's possible on the day of your excursion, get into the water, with snorkel and flippers. Just do it!

Taste Poisson Cru

This traditional Tahitian recipe is marinated, raw fish; seasoned with fresh coconut milk and lime. It's an exotic dish which tastes of island paradise. You'll find it on most restaurant menus and on the breakfast buffet at most resorts.

Because it's simply prepared with fresh ingredients, Poisson Cru is a reliably good dish to select wherever you are eating in Bora Bora. Portions are generous, and the price is moderate so it's good value, delicious, and healthy.

BORA BORA EXCURSION TIPS

Choose your Bora Bora excursions and activities
ahead of time as the best ones can be booked out,
especially during busy periods. Use these tips to
ensure you have the most fun on your Bora Bora
vacation.

Tip 1

A lagoon tour is a *must*. Take snorkeling gear as *the scenery below the water can be even more spectacula*r than that above! Gloria had never snorkeled in her life yet, the first time she put on goggles to look in the water, she was so enthralled that she forgot all her fears.

Tip 2

When you go on a lagoon excursion, don't feel shy about asking your guide if he can take you through the pass to the royal-blue ocean outside the reef. This is such an unforgettable experience and, because you're in a small boat, it's only possible when weather conditions are perfect for it. The opaque blue of the water gives visibility way into the depths and distance. You can spot some of the marine life that you would usually only see on a Bora Bora dive. If you are lucky, you'll get to see large, long, lemon sharks; gliding underneath.

Tip 3

Bora Bora tours are great fun in a small group but it's also worth paying extra for a private excursion. The cost reflects the island's remoteness (and thankfully keeps the legendary beauty pristine). This may be your only opportunity to romantically circle the world's most famous lagoon, in style, and you will replay the inner movie the rest of your life.

Tip 4

Pre-book online to save up to 30% on the cost of a tour purchased through your resort's activity desk. Resorts add 10-30% on top of the cost of each excursion they promote. By doing this you can save more than money as you will also save precious vacation time by not having to queue up at the tour desk!

Tip 5

Confirm your excursion through email the day before or ask the concierge at your hotel to call for confirmation. It's very disappointing to get up early, rush through breakfast, and sit at the dock waiting for an excursion provider that doesn't show. (We know from experience!) Even if you've had confirmation of the tour being booked, we recommend that you always reconfirm the day before.

Tip 6

The Bora Bora resorts favor certain excursion providers for more reasons than that they provide a good service. Be aware that you can choose ANY tour provider, not just the ones listed in the activities book at your hotel. Of course, you can get recommendations from the concierge if you haven't taken time to do your own research on best Bora Bora tours beforehand.

Tip 7

This is a practical tip that most ladies will appreciate. Be prepared to tie down your hair! Always take a hair elastic with you on excursions. It can be windy out on the lagoon and a scarf or well-fitting hat may *also* be useful to keep your hair under control. Make sure your hat is of a type that can withstand the wind and water. I have two extra-great hats with elastic bands at the back to tie around a pony tail – which prevents them from blowing away. A hair tie is essential when using a snorkel too.

ACTIVE BORA BORA

I f you're a type who must do something *active* every day, there are interesting ways to keep moving in Paradise. This is a water world. Fitness freaks can jump straight from their overwater bungalow to do laps in the lagoon. Bring a set of goggles for swimming.

All the resorts provide a gym for guests to use at their leisure so if you feel compelled to keep to your regular gym schedule, you'll have a state-of-the-art gym, with an inspiring view, to continue your program. You're likely to have it all to yourself when you go.

THE MOST *"ACTIVE"* RESORTS

Four Seasons Bora Bora

Four Seasons is the resort with the most on-site activities available to guests including:

- Wave runner guided tours
- Tennis lessons
- Marine naturalist experience
- Non-motorized water sports like paddle boards, kayaks, snorkeling equipment and canoes
- Yoga by the lagoon
- Fitness center

- Snorkeling in the Lagoonarium

Conrad Bora Bora

Conrad offers guests the following on-site activities:
- Snorkeling
- Mini golf
- Day trips to Motu Tapu
- Fitness center
- Non-motorized watersports including paddle boards, kayaks and pedalos
- Hobie cat sailing
- Cultural activities with the pool boys, including lessons on how to tie a pareo, do traditional Tahitian weaving, and crack coconuts

ALL ACTIVITIES AVAILABLE

We recommend that folk who *thrive on being active* book at least 2 excursions to enjoy the best that Bora Bora offers. There are many more activities available on the island than those your resort can provide. Here's a complete list:
- Snorkeling tours
- Shark & ray tours
- Motu tours
- Scuba diving
- Helmet dive
- Underwater scooter
- Snuka snorkel
- Lagoon & deep-sea fishing
- Jet boards
- Kite surfing
- Parasailing
- Skydiving
- Hobie cat sailing
- Sailing on a racing catamaran
- Sunset cruises

- Stargazing
- Motu picnic & dinners
- Photo lagoon tour
- Boat hire with or without skipper
- Yacht charter
- 4x4 Safari
- ATV excursion
- Rent a car, scooter or bike
- Seaplane tours
- Yoga
- Turtle sanctuary tours
- Day cruises
- Jetski & Raverunner tours
- Wakeboarding
- Waterskiing
- Tubing
- Whale watching & swimming
- Coral nursery tour

ACTIVITIES FOR THE ADVENTUROUS

Hike the mountain

Hiking on Bora Bora is a rewarding experience. The lush tropical vegetation is exotic and amazing panoramas can be viewed from various vantage points up at lookouts that were built during world war 11. There are two walking tracks which were used to cross the island and get from one village to the other before the Circle Island Road was constructed by U.S. soldiers in world war 11. All trails can be accomplished in a couple of days because the island is small. However, the hiking trails are only open in dry weather. To hike around Bora Bora's rugged in-land you must choose to visit over the driest months (and keep your fingers crossed). Even then you may not be able to hike as it can rain at any time of year.

Valley of the Kings

It's surprising to discover that, before missionaries came to Bora Bora, the inhabitants lived in the inner parts of the isle as that felt safer to them. The Valley of the Kings has pathways leading to recently uncovered remnants of ancient villages and maraes, which were ceremonial religious sites. You can hike through the fertile valley amongst lush tropical vegetation and find mangoes, ginger and other tropical foods that were planted by early seafaring settlers. Valley of the Kings is an easy 3-hour walk which most people can do. Ancestors Road or the Track of the Past is an easy full day tour for the fit.

Sacred Cave of Anau

The Sacred Cave of Anau is a 6-hour trek which includes some climbing so it's only for those accustomed to vigorous exertion. A challenging, steep track leads up to a cave on the side of Mt Otemanu. When heading north, this mysterious cave can be seen from the Circle Island Road, soon after Anau village!

Mountain Climbing

Up for a challenge? From below you may wonder how it's possible, but Mount Pahia and Mt Otemanu can be climbed! This strenuous feat is a dry weather activity. As soon as it rains, the unmaintained trail becomes muddy and slippery, and even experienced locals won't walk it. Seeking help from a local guide is recommended but, at present, it's not easy to find someone to take you.

Mount Otemanu Climb

Mount Otemanu (727m), the highest and most recognized feature on Bora Bora Island can only be climbed up to its "shoulders". The crumbly vertical cliffs of the towering peak prevent further ascent as they do not hold clamps. Although it has never been scaled by foot it's possible for a helicopter to land on the summit.

Mount Pahia Climb

Mount Pahia (2,168ft/661m) can be climbed in about 4 hours by fit, experienced hikers with stamina. You must only undertake this challenge in dry weather as it becomes dangerously slippery after rain. To get started, head to the Protestant church in Vaitape and take the road to the south. Follow it up until you pass clumps of mango trees and then veer towards the left. Circle the cliffs, keeping to the top of the left side.

A local guide is very useful but some of the websites offering these are outdated. The only guide we know who offers a Mount Pahia climb is Azdine, who also takes tours through the Valley of the Kings. His Mt Pahia Climb of 6 hours is for the very fit who don't suffer from vertigo. The lofty views from this steep trail are either astounding or dizzying, depending on the state of your adrenals. Recently Azdine has been unavailable. But if you are keen to hike, try and contact him to check if he will take you.

Diving

Many divers have Bora Bora on their *must dive* list! The area is famous for manta rays and sharks, and on all dives, you will see colorful hard and soft corals, teeming with reef fish. It's the quantity and diversity of marine life that attracts scuba divers to Bora Bora.

The island was formed by a volcanic eruption which fashioned a calm, clear lagoon encircled by a string of islands and coral reef. There's only one narrow pass through the reef from the Pacific Ocean.

There are many established dive sites around Bora Bora so, whatever your level of experience, there are fascinating sites to explore. The calm lagoon is perfect for beginner divers to get comfortable with the equipment and there are more technical dives outside the reef to excite advanced divers.

Organize your dive with a provider before you leave for your vacation, to get the best price possible. Once you are on Bora Bora you will pay elevated prices to arrange dives through your resort.

Best Diving in Bora Bora

Bora Bora's most popular dives include shark dives, manta ray dives, drift-through-the-pass dives and beginner coral garden dives. This is a small island so it's a quick boat trip to get to nearly all of Bora Bora's most popular diving spots. However, two of the best diving spots are only available on a private dive or through a specially organized dive trip. These more distant dive locations take up to an hour to get to but are well worth the extra time and money.

ROMANCE IN BORA BORA

You're off to the island of romance ... but don't
leave the magic to chance!
Here are the most romantic activities
that you need to book in advance.

n Bora Bora, romantic activities abound. Many are freely available with a resort-stay on the world's most mesmerizing island. But, if you want to turn the romance up a few notches, there are also extraordinary treats that can be planned.

Ladies are instinctively the romantic sex. Most of us crave romance even more than chocolate so don't put the onus, for providing romance, on your man. Be proactive by setting the scene for special moments to emerge.

Men will be pleased to know that they don't have to *think up* lady-pleasing ideas in Bora Bora. It's a "couple's" island so the resorts and activity providers are experts at creating experiences that touch the hearts of lovers. Surprise her with ideas from this short-list of the most romantic activities and you'll be certain to delight and charm her while making precious memories in a picture-postcard setting.

Dinner for two by the lagoon

Indulging in a private dinner for two, alongside the Bora Bora lagoon, is one of those fanciful experiences that are even more pleasurable than you imagine they will be. It's simply the most romantic thing you can do. A table will be set up in the location of your choice and you'll have your own "on-call" waiter to serve the food and drinks on your chosen menu.

Most Bora Bora resorts offer romantic dinners so let's take a sneak peek at the best of the best!

A romantic dinner at St Regis can be located at the main beach, spa beach, spa, or on the deck of your bungalow. On our last vacation, my boyfriend booked a dinner at the spa beach and surprised me by proposing! A romantic private dinner offers many perfect moments for delivering a Bora Bora proposal.

Dinner for two at the Four Seasons beach

Four Seasons Resort offers guests a choice of dining locations: on the main beach, in the privacy of their overwater bungalow, or on the small, secluded, nearby islet (at an extra cost).

Private lunch on the Sofitel Private Island

Luxurious tete a tete dining doesn't need to be "dinner". We experienced the lunch of our lives at the Sofitel Private Island with some of the island's most picturesque scenery in full technicolor around us.

Couples Luxury Spa Experience

The spas at Bora Bora resorts have been designed with exotic areas for relaxing, couple's experiences. If you're lucky, you might get a couple's massage as part of a package. Our savvy travel agent organized one to be added in, complimentary, on our 5-night stay at St Regis.

Four Seasons has the most lavish couple's room, with an outdoor bath and sensational views. Booking a treatment in this exclusive setting is very pricy but, if you can part with the money, you'll truly be in heavenly indulgence with your honey!

Private Lagoon Tour

For years we had supposed that we didn't need to spend on a private tour as Bora Bora looks just as beautiful on a small-group boat tour. But after we experienced the joy of a private lagoon tour, with a feet-in-the-water Polynesian picnic lunch on a motu, we discovered that having a boat and captain "just for us" made our day out much more romantic.

Sunset Tour

Reflecting reverently, side by side with your loved one, while watching the sun set is superb from anywhere on the island. But – unless you have one of the Conrad Presidential villas, with front row seats to the ocean – getting out on the lagoon for a sunset tour is another *must do* Bora Bora romantic activity.

Sailing the lagoon

Opportunities for *sailing* the lagoon are very limited and it's a sublime experience. At the time I decided to book an excursion with Vitamin Sea, the sunset cruise was sold out. But, luckily, the floating bar sailing experience was still available. This was *my* darling's favorite excursion so be sure to get in, well ahead of going, if you want to be sure of a place.

Flower-Bed Surprise

Imagine walking into your bungalow to find your bed adorned with tropical flowers and petals strewn across the floor to a bubble bath. This surprise added a delightful, romantic touch to the end of a perfect day in paradise. Staff at the Conrad Bora Bora Nui resort heard that we had become engaged, so they set this up while we were at dinner. Some packages organized through a specialist Tahiti travel agent can include a flower- bed surprise. If your package doesn't, book one at your resort. A perfect time to ask for this novel treat to be arranged is while you're enjoying a private dinner by the lagoon. Just when your darling thinks the evening is ending, it gets even more romantic!

Bora Bora Photoshoot

You're finally living your dream of a Bora Bora vacation! Capture your togetherness in Paradise by having a romantic photo shoot session with a Bora Bora photographer. The right person will help you feel so comfortable that posing with your partner will be fun and enhance your connection. On the first trip that Tom flew to Bora Bora with me I organized a photo-shoot to get myself in some photos with him. I had no idea that the shots would become my engagement photographs.

String the romance together, like pearls

Bora Bora is intoxicating. Simply sitting together watching a sunset is a romantic event wherever you are on the island. You can maximize moments by blending the most romantic activities together to create a perfect day in paradise. Try adding in a cruise on the lagoon and /or savoring a private dinner for two. How about going back to your bungalow to be surprised by a perfumed flower-bed? Imagine if this incredible evening was preceded by a couple's massage at the spa! The possibilities for heightening romance in Bora Bora are endless ...

PROPOSING IN BORA BORA

In Bora Bora you can propose with a backdrop be-fitting a great love story. It will be a moment to smile about for the rest of your lives. Here are some perfect proposal ideas, in locations so romantic they'll cast a spell over her ... ever after.

Sofitel Island Motu

The lookout at the top of the Sofitel's Private Island is the secret domain of the few travelers who stay at this boutique hotel. Wooden steps lead up through exotic tropical gardens to amazing 360-degree theatrical views over Bora Bora, Mt Otemanu, and the lagoon. An island-style shelter or a wooden viewing platform with a dramatic outlook can be used to set the scene. The Sofitel can create a romantic setting that includes fragrant flowers, champagne, and anything else that you think of to make this the most pivotal moment of your lives.

Sunset Cruise

Sailing around the gleaming lagoon, watching the sun slowly setting, is another of the most romantic things to do in Bora Bora. Book a private tour to have more intimacy while posing the question. A romantic dinner can be included to celebrate the occasion.

Over Water Bungalow

An overwater bungalow makes a romantic love-nest above the Bora Bora lagoon. To create a big impression, choose one with a view to majestic Mt Otemanu. Delight her by popping the question as you sip champagne on your deck, watching the sun set.

Dinner on the Beach

I'm one of the luckiest women on earth: I was proposed to over dinner under the stars on a Bora Bora beach! It was a perfect, balmy evening and the most romantic time of my stay. A table, decorated with flowers and candles, was set up in a secluded spot on a beautiful beach and we had our own personal waiter to serve the special menu we'd selected.

If you'd like to propose over dinner on the beach, get in touch with your resort prior to your trip and book this exclusive experience. All the best resorts offer a private dinner for two. Some resorts allow you to select a menu from options available, so you can choose dishes that you know your love will like. The larger resorts set up private dinners in a few locations around the resort: the beach, an islet off the beach, the spa grounds, or the inner lagoon; are examples. Reserving your dinner well ahead of time ensures you have first pick of the best location.

A Hammock for Two

Here's a more casual suggestion for those seeking to propose somewhere "outside of the box". A few resorts have hammocks-for-two in gorgeous locations on the beach. They're simply begging for someone to come, sit a-while, and romance their honey. Pearl Beach Resort has one with a view across the turquoise lagoon to the outline of the Valley of the Kings on Bora Bora Island. My other favorite is on a sandy isle, off the beach, at the Intercontinental Resort and Thalasso Spa. St Regis offers a romantic hammock in shallow water on the beach. This makes a delightful lounger to relax in while watching the sunset.

Don't be concerned about crowds: you're likely to have the area to yourself. An astonishing thing about the perfect beaches at most of the Bora Bora resorts is that there are so few people on them. Most guests laze on the decks of their over water bungalows.

Dining at Lagoon Restaurant

Lagoon, at St Regis is the most dazzling restaurant in Bora Bora when the sky turns on a spectacular sunset with hypnotic Mt Otemanu views to match. On a lovely evening the outside deck is a romantic place to propose over cocktails or dessert. Who could murmur anything but "yes"!

Private Island Picnic

Take your love on a private lagoon tour that includes a lunch of fresh island specialties, on a private motu. This gives time to linger over a lunch with your feet in the water and then relax on a quiet beach overlooking the lagoon and Bora Bora Island. You'll be sure to find the right moment to ask.

Your Romantic Resort

The best Bora Bora resorts can arrange an intimate, romantic dinner for you, either privately in your bungalow, or in a location around the resort.

- Intercontinental Thalasso has an intimate outdoor pavilion with a grand view over the lagoon.
- St Regis and Four Seasons have butlers that are dedicated to helping you with wants and whims throughout your stay. If you need help in planning proposal ideas, we recommend contacting them prior to arrival. The St Regis has a dedicated romance butler for organizing engagement and wedding events.
- Sofitel Private island has one of the most beautiful locations for a private lunch or dinner on the beach.
- Pearl Beach resort has a lovely beach-side location for a private meal that can be especially arranged as a surprise for your loved on.

Spontaneity is Special Too

Don't let us tell you how to propose in Bora Bora. The tropical infusion of lush beauty, island scents, and warm air, may create a moment of such intimacy that you look into her eyes and know it's the time. Your sincerity and spontaneity will touch her heart. Bora Bora has all kinds of proposal stories.

FAMILY FRIENDLY BORA BORA

Where else in the world can adventurous children
swim safely with graceful sharks and pat stingrays
like
puppy dogs?

Thinking of going to Bora Bora with kids? It's a fantastic place for a unique family vacation. Where else in the world can children swim safely with graceful sharks, pat stingrays like puppy dogs, or begin snorkeling in a warm lagoon right outside their door! A *Bora Bora* family vacation is unique.

Fortunately, some hotels know that not everyone makes it to Bora Bora for their honeymoon and even those who do may want to return later, with their children.

TRAVELING WITH SMALL CHILDREN

Resort accommodation in Bora Bora is nothing like a typical hotel suite. You're coming to a destination where most rooms are surrounded by water. Bora Bora is famous for its overwater bungalows but they are not ideal accommodation for minding babies, toddlers, and young children that can't swim. Many of us come from a country with strict laws requiring fences and gates around swimming pools.

It may surprise you that the overwater bungalows in Bora Bora have decks without railings: once the balcony door is open, there is nothing to stop your child from falling into the lagoon.

Most resorts don't want guests to book an over water bungalow if they have small children and if parents do, they will ask you to sign a waiver when checking in.

You don't want to spend your vacation worrying so the best accommodation for those traveling with small children is a beach or garden bungalow. These Bora Bora resorts offer on land accommodation that is great for young children:

- Four Seasons have luxury on-land villas with 2 or 3 bedrooms.
- St Regis has Reef Side Garden Villas, Pool Beach Villas and a huge walled-in Royal Oceanfront Retreat Villa with 2 bedrooms.
- Le Meridien Resort has Pool Beach Villas with 1 or 2 bedrooms.
- Pearl Beach Resort has Garden Pool Villas and Otemanu View Beach Suites.
- Conrad Bora Bora Nui offers more choices for on-land accommodation options than any other resort. Choose from a King Garden View Suite, King Beach Pool Villa, King Garden Villa, King Horizon View Villa, King Lagoon View Suite or a Twin Lagoon View Suite.
- Intercontinental Le Moana has beach bungalows.

Be aware that many of the on-land options also have a pool, a spa, or the beach is just a few meters away. You will need to be diligent in keeping an eye on your children – which is why a family friendly hotel is best for giving *every* member a great vacation.

However, if you have children that can swim, they will love jumping into the water from your over water bungalow and you can choose whatever room style you like.

TOP 3 FAMILY-FRIENDLY HOTELS

These hotels are the best at entertaining and catering for children:

1.Four Seasons Bora Bora

Those who have stayed at a Four Seasons hotel will know that family friendliness is not just a marketing concept, it's evident all around. In accord with this paradigm, the Bora Bora Four Seasons oozes romance, yet also shines as one of the most family friendly resorts. It's a tropical playground with fun for everyone.

Four Seasons has a history of attracting more vacationers with children than any other on the island. (One family has even returned every year during the 8 years that the resort has been open.) The hotel is flexible about the number of people in an overwater bungalow when the occupants are two adults with children. Families also have the option of booking an on-land villa with 2 bedrooms and bathrooms, if more space is desired.

Kids Have Their Own Space and Adventures

The Four Seasons kid's club is available any day that a child wishes to participate. If there are "keen to come" children staying at the resort it will automatically open each day. When your children are the only ones at the resort, the kid's club will be on-call for the times you want them to attend: you can drop your kids off during the day at any time, with short notice.

In "kid space" children listen to Polynesian legends and learn traditional crafts: flower-crown weaving, basket weaving, coconut painting, and pareo painting. They are also taken fishing, go on island scavenger hunts, and can enjoy the water-playground next to the purpose-built children's room.

There's a babysitting service available for little ones (4 years and under) and you can book after hours care for other children too.

Complimentary Activities and Care

- Paddle boards and kayaks are complimentary at the Four Seasons and there always seems to be plenty waiting on the beach. This enables whole families to paddle out together. You can paddle for as long as your kids want, every day, without thinking about hourly hire charges.
- The lovely pool at the Four Seasons Bora Bora is very kid friendly as it has a sloping, shallow end that gradually deepens.
- Older children will be thrilled by jumping from the private pontoon of their overwater bungalow, even if you stay a whole week.
- The lagoonarium beach at Four Seasons is a perfect place for children to walk into the water on sloping sand and get comfortable with their mask and snorkel.
- Sunscreen is available at convenient stations around the property, as is cool drinking water.

- A laundry bungalow, with washing machines and clothes dryers, is located on each pontoon for guest use. This means you can bring less with you and wash as you need.

If your Bora Bora vacation package includes breakfast – and if you book through the right travel agent, it will – then your children's breakfast will also be included. There's a large choice of kid friendly foods like bacon, eggs any style you want, crepes, waffles, pancakes, fresh fruit, pastries, and juice. Even fussy eaters will find breakfast a highlight of their day. At lunch and dinner time there's a special children's menu offering well-priced, kid-approved options including chicken, hamburgers, mahi mahi fish, fruit salad and French fries.

The Four Season's Employees

The staff at Four Seasons are happy and guest focused, which is exactly what parents need on a vacation in Bora Bora with kids. Whilst some resorts employ on a one-year contract, at Four Seasons, when the probation period has passed workers can stay indefinitely. So most actually live on the world's most beautiful island and build relationships with their team.

From the exciting boat arrival to the sad goodbye, the Four Seasons is a family friendly Bora Bora resort. The warm, thoughtful staff welcome children and give the whole family a memorable experience. The rates might seem more than other Bora Bora resorts but there are goodies added in for free – water activities, kid's breakfast, laundry, sunscreen, and kids club supervision and activities. The children's meals are cheap – around $12 a meal. Taking kids along won't add much to the overall cost of your trip and they will enjoy the resort as much, or even more, than you!

2. Conrad Bora Bora Nui

After a complete revamp, the Nui – which some may remember as a Hilton – has reopened as a Conrad. It's now a stunning 5-star resort that's perfect for couples *and* the few families who come to Bora Bora with kids.

A Dedicated Kid-Space

A colorful indoor children's area has been created, next to the gym. Play areas have been set up, and a fully-supervised daytime program of activities, like that offered at Four Seasons, is being implemented. There's a cute outside playground for littlies, just a few steps from the door.

Best Bora Bora beach for kids

Nui's sandy beach makes a perfect playground for kids and no matter how busy the resort is, the beach is so long that you'll always find a spot that you can have all to yourselves. The shallow water along the beach has a smooth bottom – unlike most other resorts, which have small pieces of broken coral in the water. There's an amazing stretch of coral, right along the beach, just a few meters from the water's edge. Kids with water confidence can have the time of their lives snorkeling to sight different types of colorful, tropical fish. Small children can sit at the water's edge and watch curious, neon fish darting around their legs.

Complimentary Activities

- Some of the best snorkeling to be found anywhere in Bora Bora lies just a few meters off the beach and around the overwater bungalows. This is the only resort on the island with such easy access to superb snorkeling.
- A variety of water equipment awaits guests and there's always a choice of craft, sitting right on the beach. The whole family can take pedalos, kayaks or paddle boards out on the lagoon or book a sail in a hobie cat with a skipper.
- A mini-golf course, set between palms, was available every time we rode past.

More Accommodation Choices

This resort has 2 newly constructed *beach* bungalows, just a few steps from a quiet part of the beach which is hiding some of the best snorkeling in Bora Bora. The *garden* and *hillside* bungalows have been completely refurbished, with a light and airy "look and feel" and offer a little more space than the regular overwater bungalows. Families have a choice of accommodation styles on land if they prefer not to be over the water with young children. For those desiring more space, the luxurious Presidential and Royal overwater bungalow villas provide 2 or 3 bedrooms and bathrooms to match. The Presidential villas are ideal for a family with older children as there is complete privacy between bedrooms; and large, separate recreation areas.

3. St Regis Bora Bora

St Regis doesn't promote itself as "family friendly" and mostly attracts honeymoon couples but does provide an unsupervised, indoor children's play-room. St Regis can be considered for a family vacation, but your children will probably be the only ones there.

Complimentary Activities

- The protected lagoon at St Regis is the best on the island and "looking for Maeva" (a huge turquoise napoleon fish) will likely be the favorite activity of children who can swim.
- The main pool has a shallow end where parents can relax in comfort while watching a young one.
- Older kids can safely enjoy riding bicycles around the vast grounds as staff driving the small golf carts are vigilant in giving bikes and walkers the right-of-way. If you have a child too young to ride, you can have a basket seat for your little one to sit on the back.
- Kayaks and stand-up paddle boards are available on the main beach.

Spacious accommodation

St Regis has the largest bungalows in Tahiti. Families may want to take advantage of their size because the generous space makes the bungalow easy for a family to share. In an overwater bungalow the bedroom and the huge, living room are separated by a hallway, so the kids can be in one room and the parents in another. Or for more space, the 2 bedroom on-land reef and beach villas, with private pools, are even more roomy than the overwater villas; and are terrific value.

AFFORDABLE FAMILY-FRIENDLY!

If you're seeking a moderate-priced option for a family vacation, Le Meridien is the best choice. This resort may not offer the top luxury of those above, but the view across to Mt Otemanu – from the restaurants, pool, and beach – is as good as it gets! The modern, one and two-bedroom beach villas are in a great location for children to play right outside the door. They're a much more affordable price for a vacation with kids.

Le Meridien Resort has two pools, a large beach, and a protected inner-lagoon that's a safe place to snorkel with kids. A highlight of a Le Meridien stay is the turtle sanctuary. A marine biologist gives educational talks about the turtles and guests can book to swim with them too. This is an intriguing activity for children of all ages. There is no kid's club at Le Meridien, but babysitting can be organized. Children's meals, movies, and activity packs are also available.

THE BEST ACTIVITIES FOR KIDS

Snorkeling

- The Four Seasons Resort has the perfect place for children to learn to snorkel. The inner lagoon has a sandy beach where children can get acquainted with their snorkel gear. As they extend their comfort zone, they can gradually venture out deeper to see fish and coral.
- Older children, who are competent swimmers and familiar with their snorkels, can be taken on a lagoon excursion to visit coral gardens around the lagoon. They will be enthralled by swimming with reef sharks, patting sting-rays, searching for manta rays, and visiting the most abundant coral gardens in the lagoon. An excursion which includes a motu picnic will give kids a taste of island life and Polynesian culture. This fun day out will be the highlight of their vacation.

Half-day Snorkeling Tour

- Taking this four or five-hour trip around the island is the most exciting thing to do in Bora Bora and the time will go very fast. You will swim with sharks, pat string rays and see the tropical fish and coral gardens. Consider booking a longer tour with a motu picnic that the kids will enjoy.

Jet Ski & ATV Tour

- If your kids are old enough and adventurous, take them on a jet-ski tour around the lagoon. An adult will need to drive the jet-ski, but the kids can come along for the ride. ATV is a fun way to tour the main island around the Circle Island Road with older kids.

Turtle Sanctuary

- Kids of all ages will enjoy a visit to the Turtle Sanctuary at Le Meridien resort. If you are not staying at the resort, contact Le Meridien ahead of time to organize a day visit which will include boat transfer to and from the resort. Go during the morning when the turtle feeding session takes place, it's an interesting and informative experience. Spend at least a half day at the resort enjoying their lagoonarium and consider booking a time to swim with turtles on a guided tour.

Glass Bottom Boat Tour

- Those with littlies who are too young to swim will enjoy a tour of the lagoon in a glass bottom boat. The whole family can see the colorful marine life, without even having to get wet. The water is usually so clear that the visibility for sighting coral and fish will be very good.

Lagoonarium Visit

- Arrange a visit to the Lagoonarium, managed by three Polynesian brothers, to give kids an up-close and personal encounter with marine life in a more controlled environment. You can even have the experience of being pulled along by a lemon shark – while closely supervised by a guide. The Lagoonarium is located on a motu on the eastern side of Bora Bora so you will need to book a visit, ahead of going, to have transport arranged.

TIPS WHEN TRAVELING WITH KIDS

- If your children intend snorkeling, make sure you get them well-fitting gear before leaving home. The Four Seasons has quality children's snorkel sets, but if you are at any other resort, we strongly suggest you bring your own.
- Bring flippers for snorkeling, to assist your kids in keeping pace with the group. Flippers don't only give propulsion, they also make it easy to float.
- Bring refillable water bottles for the kids. If you are staying at a 5-star resort, the evening maid who attends to your villa is likely to leave as many bottles of water as you request. (You may need to hold up fingers to communicate.)
- Sunscreen is readily available around the pool and beach areas at 5-star resorts. Bring your own to take on excursions outside the resort.
- The Four Seasons provides washing machines near the bungalows, which means you can pack less clothes. Conrad also has laundry facilities available. The St Regis offers butler service to have clothes cleaned (at a cost). However, your kids will practically live in swimmers on this warm, water vacation!
- Request a room located close to the resort facilities. If you are too far from the center of the resort, it's not so kid-friendly.
- Bring reef shoes for the kids. Most of the beaches in Bora Bora have pieces of broken coral, which may be sharp, lying in the water. Reef shoes are also practical anytime you're not wearing flippers when snorkeling and going on shark and ray feeding tours.

THE PERFECT WEEK IN BORA BORA

Make the most of each moment by planning each day. Activities with an * must be booked before you go, to ensure availability.

Day 1

Fly into Bora Bora on an early morning flight (if possible). In Papeete, be ready to move promptly when boarding is called for the flight so that you can sit on the left side of the plane. If the wind is blowing in the usual direction, the left side has the best views as the pilot brings the plane in to land on the small airport-isle rimming the lagoon.

Within a few minutes of arriving you will have collected your luggage, received a warm, floral welcome, and be sitting on a shuttle-boat heading to your resort. It's useful to know that all the top resorts have transit rooms for the convenience of the guests who arrive early or depart late. If your room isn't ready you can use comfortable facilities to change, shower, store luggage and begin your vacation. *Pack anything you may immediately need at the top of your bag.* There are plenty of activities to do – or sun lounges to do nothing on! Staff will let you know when your room is ready.

Enjoy the first day romping around your amazing resort. In Bora Bora, the resort grounds are like Disneyland for adults. Go exploring to discover what's around the next corner! Check out what daily activities are available during your stay and take note of the day and time that those you are interested in are scheduled. Find out what night each restaurant is open and book your dinners.

If you are feeling jet-lagged on your first day, hang by the beach or the pool. Those who have a long way to travel might like to arrange a spa treatment* for arrival day, to recover with a pampering.

After you check into your bungalow, you're likely to while away the afternoon enjoying its delights. Jump off the deck or swim in your pool, then order room-service to eat lagoon-side on your deck. Relax and unwind until it's time to glam up for a romantic stroll to your first dinner at one of the resort's restaurants.

Day 2

Take the morning to relax. Sleep in or enjoy a bath-with-a-view in your bungalow. Stroll or ride a bike to the breakfast buffet. Linger over selections and taste foods that you fancy. The best resorts offer specialty hot dishes with eggs, crepes and pancakes, that can be freshly made to your liking. So do remember to try the a-la-carte menu that's also available. Choose from the made-to-order drinks which include fruit juices and milk shakes.

After breakfast take out a paddle board, kayak or canoe.

Enjoy lunch, lagoon-side, by ordering room-service to deliver to your overwater bungalow. Your server will arrive with a hot/cold cart and set up the table on the deck of your bungalow.

After lunch visit the resort's lagoonarium or beach to get comfortable in the water with your snorkeling equipment.

Day 3

Get up in time to enjoy breakfast before heading off on a circle island tour* which includes snorkeling adventures. As the sea-life in the lagoon is most active in the morning it's the best time to see as many interesting creatures as possible. Choose a tour that includes a motu picnic.

The tour provider will drop you back at your resort and you will probably want to relax for the remainder of the afternoon. Visit the pool for afternoon snacks and cocktails.

Day 4

Reserve this day for lounging around the resort and being pampered. Engage in any complimentary activities on offer. Have a hit of tennis, mini golf, table tennis or billiards.

Visit the spa facilities and experience a Polynesian massage* or body scrub*. This island is a great place to indulge in a couple's spa experience*. You can both unwind in an extraordinary tropical setting and not have to break state by driving home afterwards.

Complete the day with a private dinner-for-two* on the beach. Continue the intimate, connective mood by returning to your bungalow to find a romantic flower bed* awaiting.

If you are someone who needs to keep active, use half of this day to take the resort's shuttle service to the main island and explore Vaitape town. Look around the market and local craft shops for unique art and souvenirs.

Day 5

After an early breakfast, head off on a half day sailing tour around the Bora Bora lagoon, with a floating bar experience*.

When you are dropped back at the resort, enjoy lunch by the pool or on the beach. Have dinner at your resort's specialty restaurant.

Day 6

Arrange a time to meet the photographer (you have chosen) for a 2-hour professional photoshoot* at your resort. Book a morning session as the lighting is often best before noon.

In the late afternoon, be picked up at your resort's dock for a sunset cruise with champagne*. We can recommend the sunset tour that includes easy logistics for eating dinner, lagoon-side, at St Marks, which is one of Bora Bora Island's most popular restaurants. You will be dropped off at St Marks after the cruise and later be picked back up and returned to your resort.

Day 7

After breakfast, pack your main bags and have them taken to storage so you are free to spend your last day as you wish. Jump off your bungalow one last time. Make sure you have tried every hammock. Lunch in your favorite location. Savor the feeling of being in Bora Bora! You can relax and make the most of every last moment as the tiny, quiet airport is just a quick boat ride away, with no traffic lights in between. If possible, book an afternoon flight to extend your hours at the resort.

There's a lot to do in Bora Bora. But – unless you are adrenaline junkies searching for thrills – don't squeeze too many activities into five or seven days. Leisurely "hanging out" on this island is spectacular too! Include a pleasant balance of *doing* and *being* and go home feeling like you've had the ultimate vacation in paradise. We hope that you can use our years of experience, to have a perfect week in Bora Bora – the first time you go!

TRAVEL INFORMATION

Getting Around

Airport Transfers

Check the transfer times that your travel agent has assigned to you before leaving for your trip. Transfer companies in Tahiti are known to pick guests up very early for airport departures. Even 3 hours early! You need to check this before you depart as most arrivals into Tahiti are in the middle of the night so when you find out it is too late to change the transfer time as offices are closed. We've experienced being the first people to arrive in the departure hall with a very early pick up that meant we couldn't stay to enjoy breakfast at our lovely Tahiti hotel. Instead we waited a very long time in the very small airport until our flight departed. And on our last vacation, being there that early did not assist us getting on the plane first to choose the best seats. All passengers have arrived by that time and there were about 20 people that managed to jump on the queue before us. Don't start your Bora Bora trip this way. Spend your time enjoying breakfast instead of waiting at the airport. If your transfers are going to be a silly time, consider taking a taxi to the airport instead. The resorts close to the airport are only 5-15 minutes away so there's no reason to be picked up too early for your flights. Check the actual transfer times from your hotel.

When you arrive in Bora Bora your resort will pick you up from the airport in their fancy boat (for a fee) and zip you straight to the resort. There is a free shuttle that goes into Viatape town but if you are on a motu resort the best way to have the quickest, smoothest arrival is to take the resort shuttle.

Taxis

Taxis in Bora Bora are a bargain way to get around. We think they are the best value in Bora Bora. On our last trip our taxi driver waited for our late arrival on the

Conrad boat. Then she took us and 8 bags to our Matira Beach resort for only $20. That taxi ride was the best value we had in Bora Bora - $20 for us and 8 bags! She even stopped for us to take photographs and gave lots of information on the way.

Some of the best island drivers speak great English, are very friendly, and can give interesting information as you get around the island. We've also had some who speak no English at all. Our favorite taxi driver – Vaina - also does private Circle Island Tours, in her airconditioned van, for a very reasonable price. When you are on-island phone 8773 7331 to book her wonderful service.

THINGS TO BEWARE OF IN BORA BORA

We want you to enjoy every moment in Bora Bora so be aware of the following:

Sea Urchins

You are unlikely to encounter a spikey sea urchin in Bora Bora but do be aware of them. They grow in coral reefs or around ledges in the water. Inspect the area near your bungalow before climbing into the lagoon and stepping around. Make sure you are not spiked by the protective spines on this little creature.

Fire Coral

Fire coral does grow in the coral gardens around Bora Bora. You can recognize it by the yellow-green tinge of its appearance. Touching fire coral gives a sting that can remain sore for several days. When you are in the water all coral should be avoided, not just fire coral. The coral eco system is very fragile and standing on or touching coral can hurt it. Avoid a fire coral sting by simply respecting all coral. Sometimes it is necessary to step around in the lagoon so, anytime you're not wearing flippers, have reef shoes on hand to avoid accidently contacting coral with your feet.

Hotel Phone Calls

Don't get stung by an unexpected phone bill, at check-out time! Using a Bora Bora resort phone is extremely expensive, even for local calls. The explanation given by reception is that Bora Bora has only one phone provider. I made a few local calls and incurred a charge of several hundred dollars. When I complained, it was cut in half but I still didn't smile. One way to avoid this is to buy a phone card and use the public phones while in Vaitape. The best option is to communicate by internet.

Termites & Mosquitoes

Unfortunately, even paradise has some imperfections. Although the island of Bora Bora has no poisonous snakes or spiders, it is home to some annoying creatures – mosquitoes and termites.

The 5-star resorts spray for mosquitoes so their presence is limited. However, depending on where you are in the resort and where you travel to on the island, you may wander into mosquito territory.

Staying in an overwater bungalow will reduce your exposure to mosquitoes. But be careful when you are around the edges of the resort or near dense foliage areas. Use insect repellant if necessary. Resorts like the Conrad and Pearl beach have more mosquitoes around as they are set on lush, green islands while the Four Seasons and St Regis are on flat sandy motus.

When you venture out of your resort be aware that there will be more mosquitoes around other parts of the island.

If you are traveling during the summer, wet season, mosquitoes are at their peak. Ensure you pack some effective insect repellant to protect yourself.

The bungalows in Bora Bora are built using traditional techniques and materials. While we love staying in these Polynesian huts, unfortunately, so do termites! Termites are everywhere in the tropics and the extensive use of beautiful, natural materials around the resorts means that they are facing a constant battle to keep the termites at bay.

Resorts replace the roofs of their bungalows regularly to keep them termite free and looking their best. But there is a possibility that you may encounter signs of termites in your bungalow. If you find sand-like droppings around your bungalow, they are from termites. Simply alert the resort and they will either change your room (if possible) or come to spray the room.

WHAT TO TAKE TO MAKE YOUR TRIP

FOR WOMEN

Pack a few skimpy summer dresses, skirts, shorts and tops. The air temperature in Bora Bora is so perfect in the mornings that you can even reach for a little sun dress to slip on before breakfast.

The magical, balmy evenings in Bora Bora invite you to stroll around the lush gardens and along the beach or enjoy delicious Tahiti cocktails at your resort's bar before or after dinner. In this relaxed atmosphere you can dress as casually as you like and choose an informal dining venue. But the beautiful resorts also provide romantic backdrops for dressing as exotically or elegantly as you want! There is something 'magic potion like' about the Bora Bora island ambiance. I feel like a princess, every evening I am staying in this paradise.

FOR MEN

For all those accustomed to wearing suits and ties, your Bora Bora vacation will be a dream come true. You can veg out in casual, comfortable cotton T-shirts and cotton shorts or hang in your swim shorts much of the day. Bring some long pants and romantic cotton shirts for evenings if you are staying in a classy resort or planning to visit some of best Bora Bora restaurants and/or seduce your woman. She's worth it!

For Footwear

Shoes can add weight and take up space in a bag so be aware that you will need very little footwear on this tropical, beach vacation. **Sandals and thongs will be most comfortable around your resort** and for activities like shopping. You'll mostly be walking on sand and wooden pontoons with cracks between boards – or riding bikes – so flat footwear is preferable.

Check out the Bora Bora tours on land to decide what activities you want to do. **If you plan on inland hiking you will need sneakers or rubber soled walking shoes.**

For Winter

In the section on the Bora Bora weather we reminded folks living in the northern hemisphere that they are coming to the opposite season. We also described how pleasant Bora Bora's winter temperatures actually are. But as the trade winds blow in winter, it's useful to have a **wind proof jacket** on-hand. The evenings can be a little cooler so take a shawl, **light cardigan or jacket** to be comfortable in an airconditioned restaurant or out on a boat for a sunset tour.

For the Beach

Take a few swimsuits (swimmers, bathers, boardies) to ensure you always have dry ones to put on.

We are adamant that anyone who doesn't jump in to the water at every opportunity is missing out! The lagoon is like an enormous, natural swimming pool and everywhere you look (including under-water) is a potential "screen saver". Even at the end of the on-land Bora Bora tours for exploring the island you may be dropped off at Matira Beach for a couple of hours. It happened to me. So, our number 1 tip for Bora Bora is: 'Always wear your swimsuit'. Often this means at-the-ready under your clothes. Walking around wearing your swim-wear in non-swimming environments is not considered good etiquette in French Polynesia.

Take comfortable reef shoes. They are essential for protecting your feet from small pieces of coral that may be lying on the sandy floor. The water is calm and warm thanks to the coral reef surrounding the lagoon but pieces break off. Wear reef shoes when swimming without flippers.

Bring Sun Protection

Except during Bora Bora's winter, the tropical sun can burn in minutes during the middle of the day, especially in summer. Don't spoil any moments of your vacation by frying yourself. Consult our informative Bora Bora weather page to understand how the seasons in Bora Bora can affect your vacation. We find that during winter, when the rays of the sun are less direct, fewer precautions are necessary. With light tans, we can be in the sun for an hour or two without burning. Here are our recommendations on what to take to Bora Bora for maximizing your time in the sun:

- Take a practical hat that scrunches up in your bag and un-crunches when you put it on. Your hat will be your best friend, and with all the water activities, it will likely be introduced to the lagoon sometime. Every day will be "hat day" so you may also want a stylish one for lounging about the resort.

- The Australian secret for indulging in swimming, surfing and snorkeling for hours, without burning, is to wear a "rashie". In our beach culture wearing a rashie (rash vest or rash guard) has been made cool by the sun-bleached surfies. I recommend that you purchase a rashie so that you can relax in the water. We even take long sleeved rashies in summer as the water temperature is so perfect that we want to extend our time in it. In Bora Bora, we are commonly asked: 'Where can I buy one of those?' You can now buy gorgeous women's rash guards in swimsuit shops and online. It's worth every cent to ensure you don't spend your vacation in sunburn pain.

- Women wear trendy board shorts too. Boardies (board shorts) are fantastic for protecting tender skin at the top of thighs, while snorkeling.

- Pack lots of quality sunscreen. As you will smother this all over yourself (and your sweetheart), it's preferable to **buy a nontoxic sunscreen**. Research has shown that damage done to skin by one ubiquitous sun filtering agent, commonly used in regular brands, is actually increased through exposure to sunlight!

Insect Protection

Much of the time you will be in a no-mosquito zone. The resort you choose will be close to salt water and water activities and excursions will entice you most days. The absence of mosquitoes is a big benefit of having an over water bungalow stay.

Any on-land villas, situated away from the beach, will have mosquitoes around them once the sun sets. Be prepared. Mosquito repellent is also essential when you take inland adventure tours through tropical vegetation. Buy a **non-toxic insect repellent** to take.

For Snorkeling

We advise everybody to **take quality goggles, snorkel and flippers** on their Bora Bora vacation. Ladies, this includes you, even if you've never used them before so get used to the notion of sporting casual "beach" hair. Look at the spectacular Bora Bora snorkeling experiences waiting for you and you will understand why.

Although the resorts and tour providers offer goggles and snorkels it's preferable to having your own comfortable, well-fitting gear that's not moldy and doesn't leak. Your snorkeling gear will accompany you everywhere. While you are at the sports store, buy a handy draw-string, mesh carry bag that allows it to dry off after use.

Carry Bags

Bring a water-proof back pack or tote bag for day excursions. It's also ecological to bring your own carry bags for shopping. The islands of Tahiti are very small and garbage must be kept to a minimum. To comply with this policy, shops do not give out shopping bags, they must be purchased.

Alcohol

The cost of alcoholic drinks is quite high in the bars at Bora Bora resorts. You may want to bring some of your favorite bottles to relax over drinks on the deck of your villa. If you have a ViniBag - a reusable, inflatable travel bag you can pack your favorite bottles in your suitcase and bring them from home. Those who stop in Papeete, on their way through to Bora Bora, can have a different experience shopping at a Carrefour supermarket in Papeete. They stock a wide variety of alcohol and you can purchase some delicious liqueurs with flavors such as vanilla and coconut, that are made in Tahiti.

What to Take for a Cruise

Tahiti cruise ships have extensive air conditioning throughout their rooms. In your cabin you can set the temperature for your personal comfort. But, if you are sensitive to cold, you will need light cardigans or jackets in some of the public areas, especially in the dining rooms and theaters.

WHAT NOT TO TAKE TO BORA BORA

When deciding what to take to Bora Bora you can happily **forget your jewelry.** You'll see Tahitian women displaying their artistic shell bracelets and necklaces and want to adorn yourself "island style".

You can have a lot of fun and romance shopping for pretty pieces of Tahitian jewelry, both pocket friendly and precious. Tahiti pearls can be found in every price bracket. Over the rest of your life they will provide tangible memories of your romantic Tahiti vacation.

Made in the USA
Middletown, DE
25 May 2020